CHOICES

AND

Challenges

JANET RENO
11200 NORTH KENDALL DRIVE
MIAMI, FL 33176

Mr. Alan Greer
201 South Biscayne Blvd.
Miami, Fl

Dear Alan:

I have just finished Choices and Challenges, Faith, Hope and Love. It is one of the most interesting and thought provoking books I have read on that which puzzles us all - "God, people, life itself and how they all tie together." As a student of the Bible and the human condition on earth, you write eloquently about the need for each of us to assume personal responsibility for better understanding and pursuing God's plan for us.

You make clear that what is important is not wealth and acclaim but "how well we live our lives and the choices we make in giving our love, as God has taught us, to those who touch us day in and day out and who we touch in return – our families, friends, community, society and world."

Sincerely,

Janet Reno

המשנה לראש הממשלה
VICE PRIME MINISTER

May 4, 2005

Choices and Challenges, Faith Hope and Love

Choices and Challenges is a beautifully written and powerful exploration of humanities relationship with God and each other. Alan Greer argues forcefully for religions and multiplicity of racial as well as ethnic grouping in order to advance humanity into a better future which only God can fully foresee.

Shimon Peres

CHOICES

AND

Challenges

LESSONS IN FAITH, HOPE AND LOVE

ALAN G. GREER

New York

Choices & Challenges
Lessons in Faith, Hope, and Love

Softcover ISBN 978-1-60037-551-4

Hardcover ISBN 978-1-60037-552-1

Library of Congress Control Number: 2008944265

MORGAN · JAMES
THE ENTREPRENEURIAL PUBLISHER

Morgan James Publishing, LLC
1225 Franklin Ave., STE 325
Garden City, NY 11530-1693
Toll Free 800-485-4943
www.MorganJamesPublishing.com

In an effort to support local communities, raise awareness and funds, Morgan James Publishing donates one percent of all book sales for the life of each book to Habitat for Humanity. Get involved today, visit **www.HelpHabitatForHumanity.org**.

To

My beloved Patricia

and her father,

Richard J. Seitz,

A true hero in every sense of the word

Acknowledgements

There is a host of those I owe a debt of thanks to in terms of the insights, ideas, and encouragement I have received in producing *Choices & Challenges*. Most especially, I want to acknowledge the invaluable help of my editor, Bruce Scali, whose efforts, suggestions, and words have made this a far better book than it would have been without him. Likewise, without the wonderful perseverance and support of my agent, Lois de la Haba, you would not be reading this.

I would be remiss if I also didn't acknowledge the invaluable help of my assistants over the years, Ivonne Silva and Bonnie Kirton. I also want to thank Denise Ackermann who read the earliest version of what became *Choices & Challenges*. Her insightful recommendations got me off on what I believe was the right foot. As to all the rest, too numerous to list here, you know who you are and have my deepest thanks.

Contents

"Remember not the events of the past,
The things of long ago consider not;
See; I am doing something new!
Now it springs forth, do you not perceive it?"
Isaiah 43:18-19

Introduction

I am an extremely fortunate man. But it's not the fair share of earthly rewards and accolades to which I refer; God's spiritual blessings are the real measure of my riches.

Over many decades, His hand has placed me in a number of unique positions that allowed me to observe and participate in historical events that shaped the world. It turns out they were a gift that put what's really important into sharp relief; I came to realize that the frenzy and turmoil of human interaction on a grand scale were a metaphor for the quest for meaning that goes on inside all of us. The seeds for mine was planted in me as a young boy.

God had been around all my life but it wasn't until middle age that I started to pay serious attention to Him. His blessings were answers to the questions that had nettled me from the time I was an adolescent, answers that came to me when I found myself by finding Him. I'm convinced that He wants me to share my bounty with as many as I can by sharing what I have learned.

As a young Naval Officer, I served on nuclear submarines and spent a year in Vietnam during that devastating war. Later, as a trial lawyer and political activist, I participated in national political campaigns and was a part of landmark trials from Watergate to the post-2000 election cases in Florida that determined the winner of the U.S. Presidency. I've traveled Communist China before its modern opening, walked through Soweto, South Africa, during the height of apartheid, and recoiled at the reality of slums in South America.

On my journey, I have also been awestruck and enriched by the wonders of this world and of humanity, those just outside my door as well as others around the world that are known to many. At every station I've occupied along the way, I witnessed the best and worst of human conduct.

There is more that unites us than divides us.

Not content to just live my life as if it were a game of chance, winning some hands, losing others, and breaking even on the rest, I was compelled to search out what seems to me the logic, purpose, and interrelation of personal and world events. I've delved into theology, philosophy, history, and politics. On my quest for spiritual understanding, I have cross-examined, if you will, humanity as a whole to make the case that life has precious meaning for every human being.

While this world of ours seems so vast and varied, with markedly different peoples, customs, and beliefs that provide built-in excuses for conflict, I have come to realize that it is really a very small place with more that unites us than divides us.

I ask, what are the material differences between the racism of apartheid South Africa and our history of segregation in the U.S? Between the poverty of the rural Arkansas of my youth and that in South America? Between the historic fallacies that the Sun revolves around the Earth and that the Universe revolves around me? Between the idols of antiquity and the false gods of today? Between the desperation of a starving body and that of a starving soul? Amongst Moses, Christ, Mohammed, and Buddha?

What do you do when things like life don't make sense? If you're like me, you ask questions, if not of others then at least of yourself. There are so many questions—but what are the answers? Dogma, tradition, and politics often say one thing when common sense seems to suggest another.

What are the material differences between the idols of antiquity and the false gods of today?

My experiences in life pushed, punched, and pulled at me until the world finally started making sense. After thirty-nine years of putting cases together out of competing facts and concepts so that I could present them to a judge or jury, I've come to understand that if something doesn't add up, by and large, people won't and shouldn't believe it. I've learned to set up, side by side, all the available facts the various differing parties profess are true and fit them together as if they were an enormous jigsaw puzzle. When they fit, the picture gets clearer; likewise, there are times when things just won't mesh and something has to either be set aside to be reintroduced later on or discarded. You can't just force the pieces together.

In this way, I've tried to study and understand that which has puzzled me all my life—God, people, life itself and how they all tie together. How does one make sense out of them? It may be presumptuous on my part, but my training and approach have given me a somewhat different perspective from that of many formal theologians, philosophers, and scientists who have confronted the same questions.

For example, as you will see throughout this book, I have a fascination with the life, times, and writings of St. Paul that I have studied extensively. Today, most Christians are taught that Paul wrote for the ages and that his directions to his church's members two thousand years ago are equally applicable and binding for our age. Yet, many people now find some of the things he was reputed to have said very troubling, especially where they deal with the proper places and roles of men as the dominant gender and women as subservient to them.

It seems to me, however, that Paul thought of himself as an underground, short-term operative who had to keep a beleaguered movement together and expand its numbers when its beliefs threatened the then-existing power structure and order. All the while, he awaited what he understood to be the imminent return of God and His rule to Earth.

If something doesn't add up, people shouldn't believe it.

Apparently, juggling was one of Paul's many talents. On the one hand he, on behalf of God and Christ, professed the impotence of the reigning gods and declared that, in a society based on slavery and female subjugation, slaves and women would soon be equal to or better than their male masters. What he advocated was a huge threat to the accepted formal structure of a then-pagan world. On the other hand, Paul counseled his flock to accept short-term accommodations, including male dominance and female subservience that were necessary for a weak and dispersed Christian community to survive until its leader's return. That return, he believed, would herald the destruction of the hostile world structure that opposed and oppressed the nascent Christian Church and set up a new world where the relations of its inhabitants, male and female, would be in a proper balance, equitable for all.

It seems to me that some of us, however, take Paul's short-term counseling and recommended accommodations and turn them into immutable laws for eternity. For this reason, I think his writings must be read in the context of his time and his purpose instead of thinking that he had at least two thousand years of future humanity in mind as he penned every word. We must, therefore, decipher what is relevant today among his writings and what is not.

A Seed Was Planted

Choices & Challenges represents my personal quest for understanding the disquieting issues that have reared their heads in ways I couldn't ignore and that quest turned out to be a journey of faith. It's the sprout of the seeds that had been planted in me long before. It responds to those who would reject God's existence as well as to those who preach outmoded dogma. But it also reaffirms that faith as God intends it exists in every venue, from a small country church to the conning tower of a nuclear submarine to the halls of Congress. Most important, it exists in everyone's heart.

What you are about to read are one person's considerations of bedeviling questions related to social discourse and faith, and the answers he uncovered. Whether one believes in God or not, it's an attempt to make some sense out of life. You may agree with what follows or you may not—in a sense, you are part of a jury hearing my case.

I was born in 1939 in Arkansas where parts of my family had lived for nearly a hundred years and I spent a number of my boyhood summers there. My rearing took place in northern Virginia until we moved to Miami for my father's health shortly before he died when I was fifteen. Other than my time at the Naval Academy and military postings later on, the only time I lived outside of Florida after that was the year after Dad's death when we returned to Arkansas to be near our extended family. However, though we loved our Arkansas relatives and friends dearly, my mother, sister, and I had been more comfortable away from small-town life in the South where the thought patterns of those around us were fixed and where mom struggled to earn a living. So we returned to south Florida.

Moral issues are always more complex than they seem.

It was in those three states that I benefited from a public, although segregated, education. The complexities of experiencing racism from the white side of the fence raised the first vague, yet troubling, moral issues of my life. My father telling me when I was eleven years old that I should always be helpful and polite to "Negroes," but never say "Sir" or "Ma'am" to them, and working on an uncle's farm with a black hand who couldn't read produced the first chinks in my comfortable understanding of the world. Later, when I drove my aunt who was a nurse across the tracks in the little Arkansas town where we lived so she could, without pay, sit up all night tending to a deathly ill black baby who was barred from the area's one, whites-only, hospital when I knew she heartily approved of such segregation, those cracks widened.

In my early teens, I watched my father suffer the agonies of crippling arthritis and psoriasis without being able to help. His endless search for relief from excruciating pain ultimately led him to the untested, but doctor-approved, experimental drug therapy that destroyed his immune system and killed him. Dad's death when I had barely turned fifteen forced me to come to grips with questions of life's unfairness and of being a "man."

I pushed these issues to the back of my mind and decided I was going to be a career Naval Officer. I went to the U.S. Naval Academy at Annapolis and then spent just over six years on active duty. My first year as an officer was served on a destroyer and from there I transferred to submarines for four years, one spent on a World War II-era diesel boat and more than two on a nuclear-powered Polaris missile submarine as an assistant navigator and operations officer. For my last year of service, I volunteered for Vietnam and, with a certain amount of Navy logic or illogic, was sent there.

I wrestled with the vagaries of life.

In those six-plus years, I spent long night watches scanning the sea and heavens, riding out hurricanes and fierce north Atlantic winter gales as well as wrestling anew with the vagaries of life. (Upon graduation from sub school, three of my classmates gave up their graduation leaves to make what turned out to be the USS Thresher's last dive when she was lost with all hands. A fourth missed that final underway because he was getting married.) I passed a number of sixty-plus-day submerged nuclear missile patrols in the Pacific where I was one of three officers who would have to confirm the authenticity of a war message should it come. During those times, I was constantly aware that I might have to take responsibility for authorizing the launch of sixteen Polaris ICBMs tipped with nuclear warheads and all the devastating results that would follow, not to mention what we would probably find when and if we returned home. I was introduced to foreign lands and peoples and saw the bravery, fear, horror and destruction of war, up close and personal.

I saw the bravery, fear, horror and destruction of war up close and personal.

Shortly before going to Vietnam, I had applied to and been accepted by the University of Florida's School of Law. That move had been prompted by a rejection of my request for Admiral Hyman Rickover's nuclear-power training program and the Navy's telling me that I could anticipate ten-to-twelve more years of Polaris Missile patrols as an inertial navigation officer. To my way of thinking, once you had made one such patrol you had made them all. Besides, without being qualified as a nuclear engineer, I had no hope of a nuclear submarine command. As there was nothing new for me to look forward to in the Navy, I elected to become an attorney. Thus, I went from in-country Vietnam to Gainesville, Florida, in a twelve-day span in September of 1967. With the exploding popularity of the Pill, the nation's reaction to the war, and other social developments, that was true culture shock!

After law school, I returned to Miami to begin my career as a trial lawyer that is still ongoing. To date, my trial work has been book-ended by two historic sets of litigation: I participated in the representation of Bebe Rebozo before the U.S. Senate Watergate Committee and, to a lesser extent, in the defense of John Ehrlichman in the Watergate criminal case, and was on the Democratic Party's side of the post-2000 Presidential Election trials in Tallahassee, with their attendant media circus, that determined who won Florida's electoral votes and thus the U.S. Presidency.

I've handled diverse cases and trials and matters such as the Republic of Panama's recovery of some of the millions its dictator, Manuel Noriega, stole from that country, and mega, bet-your-company disputes, with a handful of anti-trust and libel fights tossed into the mix. I'd be remiss if I didn't add that I've also had an ongoing stream of garden variety contract disputes, and a few messy divorces that I loathed.

"We lawyers often encounter the worst people at their best and the best people at their worst."

As a trial lawyer, I have dealt with the very best and the very worst sides of human nature. I have seen the depths of greed and the heights of altruism, neither of which was necessarily on the side of a particular case I might have wished. A partner of mine summed it up for me when he said: "We lawyers often encounter the worst people at their best and the best people at their worst."

Over the years, I've been politically active as a Democrat and have participated at the highest levels of campaigns that ranged from Mike Dukakis' 1988 presidential bid to Janet Reno's 2002 run for Governor of Florida and its post-primary election debacle. Civically, I have tried to focus on three areas as a board chair or member and fund raiser: supporting public radio and television, helping the homeless, and championing the Arts.

I have issues with all denominations—none of them has gotten it quite right.

My precious blessings include almost three decades of marriage to Patricia Seitz, an extraordinary woman who let me keep my maiden name and to whom this book is dedicated. She is a United States District Court Judge, was General Counsel to former U.S. Drug Czar, Gen. Barry McCaffrey, and was the first woman to be President of the Florida Bar.

On the religious front, I was born, raised, and baptized a Presbyterian, but for the last twenty years or so I have regularly attended church with Pat, a devout Catholic. Despite this, I consider myself a firm-believing generic Christian because I have issues with all denominations—for me, none of them has gotten it quite right. That's problematical, but not significant within the scope of the real issues at our "bar."

The Seeds Sprout

If I had to single out one religious event that has had the most impact on me it would be my ten-day solo retreat in 1989 at St. Joseph's Abbey, a Trappist monastery in Massachusetts, that was arranged for me by a close friend who is a priest. That experience of extended contemplative, but not utter, silence changed my focus; it helped me learn how to listen to God instead of shouting at Him to do what I wanted.

I am a voracious reader of history, biography, fiction, politics, theology, and comparative religion. I read two pages of the Bible every night; the biblical quotations you will encounter in the following pages are taken principally from that well-thumbed book, *The New American Bible*, Catholic Edition, Thomas Nelson Publishers, 1971.

Pat and I have traveled major chunks of the world, including large parts of the U.S., Europe, Latin America, the Middle East, Asia, and Africa. We have seen Communist China before its modern opening to a market economy, have walked through Soweto, South Africa, with just a friend and a black minister as a guide during the height of apartheid, and have glimpsed the slums of South America. We have encountered poverty and want across the world firsthand, knowing we would always return to the bounty of our homeland, the United States.

There's no shame in admitting one's insignificance in relation to God.

We've also been thrilled by some of the world's greatest natural wonders, wildlife, cities, and historical sites, and we have met remarkable people everywhere. God has placed in our path an amazing array of family, friends, godchildren, and acquaintances, ranging from preachers to presidents. It has included cartoonists, authors, artists, humorists, businessmen, military personnel, farmers, jurists, theologians, politicians, and just plain folk.

We have been blessed with health and moderate wealth when so many we have encountered and loved have not been. We have been happy even as we recognized that vast sections of this world are desperate or sad. We have knocked on personal, professional, and political doors—some opened, many more remained closed. We've found, as so many others have, that when one of those doors refused to budge, another always opened, often most unexpectedly (though I'd heard and seen many times that this is how God operates).

I've been pondering the world and those who live in it ever since the end of WW II when I was six years old. I started a habit in 1984 of keeping a personal record of my thoughts that have been expanded into this work. It is hoped there are a few God-given insights within its pages.

Choices & Challenges makes no apologies for belief in God; there's no shame in admitting one's insignificance in relation to Him. Instead, this endeavor puts forth a different understanding of our relationship with Him and each other, and suggests some answers to the arguments of those who claim God does not exist. Each chapter frames a question that confronts us—believers and non-believers alike—and a challenge associated with it. They exist whether we acknowledge them or don't and we've all responded to them, consciously or subconsciously. What I've attempted to do here is bring them to the fore so that they get more of the attention they deserve. If a light goes on for you, my efforts will not have been in vain.

Peace and contentment can be found.

The choices and challenges that I've had in my encounters with faith, hope, and love brought me closer to the kind of peace and contentment that lasts. Those things can't be bought with any amount of earthly lucre. But they can be found. Much as physicists try to uncover the unifying theory that will explain all physical interactions, I offer some fresh precedents for the social and spiritual interactions that give meaning to the time we spend on Earth. I've garnered these insights on my journey through life, God's gift to each and every one of us.

ONE

Speak, or Listen—Finding Your Way

Like so many of us, I was introduced to organized religion at an early age and tolerated it as a required inconvenience throughout young adulthood. It wasn't until after I graduated from the U.S. Naval Academy that I began separating the rites and rituals of worship that had left me unfulfilled from God Himself.

Over the next twenty years, He entered my consciousness more and more often as I sought to understand how He related to me one on one and to the rest of mankind. As far back as age seven or so, I had wondered why He did not protect all of us from harm and provide answers to my questions about social inequity, injustice, and just plain unfairness that had surfaced in my mind from the time I was six. It wasn't until I was well into my forties, after what seemed like a lot of detours, that I started to make real progress on the path toward understanding. That was when I finally began approaching God in a different way; until then, I had focused on my problems and what I wanted from God, what He could do for me. After all, wasn't He supposed to provide me with a happy, healthy life and marriage and protect me from life's vicissitudes? Wasn't He there to solve the world's problems of hunger, poverty, and conflict that nagged at me and made the gains I was making in wealth and status bittersweet?

Decades went by and although my material blessings continued, my life still had more spiritual questions than I thought it should and the rest of mankind sure didn't seem to be much improved. God didn't appear to be doing a lot on either of these fronts. Then it dawned on me that I had been asking the wrong questions—I had been thinking in terms of how God should serve me! That had been my frame of reference, but I came to see that the real issue for God's children is how we serve Him and, by extension, each other. We did not create God. We did not put Him in Heaven. He is not our servant. I realized the import of the fact that it was God Who created us and everything in the Universe. It is we who are the servants placed here by Him to carry out His will. So our job is to try to understand, as best we can, what that will is and where God wants us to go.

I had been asking the wrong questions.

With this change of focus and orientation, my life and my relationship with God and others made a lot more sense on both an emotional and intellectual level. Instead of life and religion being shoved at me on a take-it-or-leave-it basis because that's just the way it is, it began to take on a more rational shape. My epiphany, though not as dramatic as St. Paul's—who God slapped upside the head one day and turned his life toward forming the early Christian Church—has led to ways of thinking about and coming to grips with a good many of the issues and fears all too many of us ignore or hide from even though they cloud great chunks of our lives. I learned it does no good to ask the "Why me?" question or why bad things happen to good people. Obviously, life happens to all of us and it includes the bad parts no matter how much we try to dodge that fact. We should focus on how and why God uses life to interact with us individually and collectively because that is the way to salvation from all of our shortcomings.

I believe God has long-range plans and goals for humanity. He wants us to grow as individuals and societies into a single "Tree of Life" that He nurtures. We start with our imperfection and work towards perfection in the hope that we can become more like Him. I don't think He preordains our every action or a precise course of human history. Instead, He has endowed us with free will and we use this independence to either advance His plan for oneness or obstruct it. God challenges us to utilize the choices He provides to advance all of humanity by improving ourselves. Such improvement comes most when we accept the challenges of spirituality and make choices that support the most worthy causes and courses of action.

I had been thinking in terms of how God should serve me!

I believe that God not only exists, He interacts in a positive way with all of us. What follows are my responsive arguments to those who declare God to be nothing more than a human delusion or myth and to those who proclaim that God long ago ordained certain sacred texts and rules that are absolute and unchangeable truth to which all else must bow, no matter what contrary facts modern circumstances and science bring to light. Some of the choices regarding faith have to do with how we worship Him, how we honor His message, how we exercise our free will in manners of observance.

We'll also explore some of the problems with the fundamentalists' approach that the Bible's words set forth the exact and unchallengeable dictates of God that may not be questioned regardless of the contrary hard facts that confront us. We'll take a hard look at the commands God has already given us via inspired Scripture to see if they still fit humanity's needs and His plan for us. This will bring us face to face with the question of whether God wants us to look only to the past and conform to the dictates He inspired in millennia gone by, or focus on the future using our freedom of choice and God-given intellects to reshape some of His prior guides to do what is best for the whole human race now.

There is enough physical and metaphysical evidence to make the case that God does, indeed, exist.

We'll likewise look at some of the arguments put forth by authors, such as Richard Dawkins, Sam Harris, and Christopher Hitchens, who are certain that there is no God and that faith itself is a destructive and evil influence on humanity's growth. These writers focus on well-documented historic abuses and misuses of faith and then extrapolate from these perversions the argument that there can be no God because a Supreme Being would not have allowed such human conduct. We will explore their proposition that because modern science cannot explain God or prove His existence, He does not exist and is only a warped construct of man's imagination.

This battle of beliefs has been going on forever and it has been said that no matter which side of the argument you come out on, faith is one of the most personal of all issues. I choose to believe in God and believe that there is enough physical and metaphysical evidence to make the case that He does, indeed, exist, whether one believes in Him or not.

I believe that God epitomizes the unity of all things, so why would the God of us all allow such a plethora of peoples, ideas, religions and political systems to flourish all over this world? Why is there such a variety of human personalities, idiosyncrasies, cultures, and beliefs that often vex or disconcert, or outright oppose, one's own? I believe, as others do, that we can overcome the challenges that such diversity represents and bring everyone closer together under God. But how can that be accomplished? What can one person do?

Why me?

In his bestselling 1982 autobiography, *Growing Up*, Russell Baker, a *New York Times* columnist, recounts with anger that had endured ever since the diabetic coma and death of his father when Baker was just five or so:

> Bessie told me about the peace of Heaven and the joy of being among the angels and the happiness of my father who was already there. This argument failed to quiet my rage.
>
> "God loves us all just like His own children," Bessie said.
>
> "If God loves me, why did He make my father die?"
>
> Bessie said I would understand someday, but she was only partly right.
>
> That afternoon, though I couldn't have phrased it this way then, I decided that God was a lot less interested in people than anybody in Morrisonville was willing to admit. That day I decided God was not entirely to be trusted.
>
> After that I never cried again with any real conviction, nor expected much of anyone's God except indifference, nor loved deeply without fear that it would cost me dearly in pain. At the age of five I had become a skeptic and began to sense that any happiness that came my way might be the prelude to some grim cosmic joke.

I thoroughly enjoyed Baker's work, and his sentiments surely resonate for many. Nonetheless, I think he misses the point.

We often miss the point.

We've all said or heard the moans, "Why did God let this happen to me? How could He do this to *me*? There can't be a God if this can happen!" Such sentiments put us at the center of creation, believing that God exists only to serve our needs and shield us from personal trauma and pain. We insist on being the focus of His attention.

Everything I've been able to observe and read indicates that this attitude has always been with us. It is exemplified in the story of Pope Urban VIII's condemnation of Galileo Galilei for heresy in 1633 because Galileo, perhaps the most brilliant man of his time and culture, had started to popularize the notion that our Earth and the other planets revolved around the sun instead of the other way around. He based this proposition on the scientific observations he had made through the telescope he had invented in 1609.

The notion that the Earth was the center of the universe was accepted by most people in the seventeenth century and was the official dogma of the Church. According to its doctrine, not only did the Sun, planets and the stars wrap themselves around this earth, but Heaven did so as well. Thus, this natural order of things placed Man at the center of God's attention. Pope Urban, in company with a majority of the rest of the Western world, could not conceive of anything more important than himself. Therefore, he denied the hard evidence produced by Galileo and others and commanded the Church's followers to do likewise.

Pope Urban could not conceive of anything more important than himself.

Because Urban and the Church were wrong, their seventeenth-century suppression of the scientific facts espoused by Galileo ultimately failed. But it died hard for exactly the same reason the concept that God's existence depends on the quality of His fulfillment of our individual needs refuses to die. In our heart-of-hearts we just cannot conceive that God might have anything more important to do than satisfy our desires. Rudimentary astronomy and mathematics—useful science—can, however, put this feeling in its proper perspective.

The simple truth is none of us matters unless everyone is given equal consideration. If we use the knowledge that the progeny of Galileo's telescope have provided, we get a totally different view of the Universe and our place in it. With modern magnification devices, we can now see outer space that is at least twenty-five-billion light years across. In that almost inconceivable volume, we've identified at least one-hundred-billion galaxies whose suns (stars) number, at a minimum, one-hundred-million-trillion (that's a 1 followed by twenty zeroes!). If only a fraction of one percent of those suns has inhabitable planets, statistical probability tells us that there are at least one billion other intelligent species spread across the cosmos who share the Universe with us and that there are a billion-billion or more other living beings who reside in our expanded neighborhood. Can you envision so much vastness and complexity as a random occurrence or a whim, or as some sort of cosmic joke to, as Russell Baker feared, keep God amused for eternity? I can't. Rather, I'm convinced God has a use and intention for the Universe and a purpose for each of us and all the species He created.

None of us matters unless all of us do.

We are no more alone in that cosmos than we are when we're shuttered in our homes. Just because we don't see anyone there doesn't mean the six billion people who inhabit the Earth with us aren't bustling about outside. It's the same when it comes to extraterrestrial life; just because our telescopes haven't advanced far enough yet to see the "whites of their eyes" doesn't mean they aren't there. In the same way our math and physics one hundred years ago predicted that Pluto had to be where it is before we actually saw it, we can now deduce the existence of life in other however-distant locales.

We just landed on Mars again and we're digging into its polar surface in a search for indications of life. The prospect of that may be as infinitesimal as the Universe is vast, but I have no problem believing that someday, on some other mission to some other part of our galaxy, our capabilities for discovery will have advanced enough to confirm what a reasonable person could conclude now about the existence of other intelligent life.

God has a purpose for each of us.

But, like the deniers in Galileo's time, some of us go on insisting that we are alone in this vast Universe. Talk about taking something on faith! If you believe, as I do, that God created the Universe, then you have to believe God is the God and Creator of everything in it—all of those galaxies, all of those suns, all of those planets, and all of those sentient creatures no matter what their physical form or intelligence is. You have to believe that God is the God of each and every one of those billion-billion-plus souls. Me the center of such vastness? Please.

It makes perfect sense to me that God would create many types of beings to serve Him as they serve themselves. The Universe has so much order amidst the diversity and so much symmetry that I find it hard not to believe that humans will some day have to get along with many other far-away living beings just as different peoples are challenged to get along here on Earth. But, first things first, and that means coming to grips with how our own corner of the Universe fits into this vast array of life.

God, of course, would have to be the God of life in all its forms and would be aware of and interested in all billion-billion souls spread across His cosmos. We are told we were created in God's image. Does that mean He is as Michelangelo depicted Him on the ceiling of the Sistine Chapel—an Old Testament gray-bearded prophet type with a stern yet loving look on His face? What about those billion other sentient species who are out there? Wouldn't they be created in His image, too, no matter what their physical appearances are? To me, this can only mean that the image we are referring to and hoping we mirror is one of attributes, of spirit. Those of us who are Christian have been taught by Jesus that "God is Spirit." [John 4:24] Thus, it is the spirit of God that we must reflect—His love, integrity, morality, steadfastness, mercy, and purpose. Those are the attributes of God we mirror, not gender or number of limbs. His spirit is what we must strive for.

And that brings us back to the individual who isn't the center of the Universe, whether that means the cosmos or a local community.

Observable facts that surround us confirm day in and day out what our true status is.

It is the spirit of God that we must reflect.

The answer to Russell Baker's implied question that so many of us share, "Why me, Lord?" and to the one posed by nonbelievers, "If God exists, why doesn't He protect and wrap each of us in cotton wool throughout our entire lives?" can be found if we listen more often and hear the words He has passed on to us.

God ensures that each of us is unique and loves each of us as individuals. He provides the opportunity to give our lives the greatest meaning possible. His love allows us the freedom to experience everything in life: happiness, sadness, exaltation, fear, pain, sickness, health, victory, and defeat—you name it. God does this so that through all of our choices and subsequent experiences we can become the very best we can be. I'm persuaded that God knows our individual limits far better than we do and, to our chagrin, He is willing to test them. As Mother Teresa is reputed to have said, "I know God will not give me anything I can't handle. I just wish He didn't trust me so much."

So where does that leave us in terms of the disquieting parts of our existence? Are we being punished for our shortcomings and misdeeds? Obviously, some of us think so. In fact, a national political figure is reported to have said in private that he blocked greater funding for AIDS research because "AIDS is God's will." This individual believes a hideous disease is God's way of scourging sinners and purging evil elements from the Earth. If we follow that train of thought, we would be thwarting God's will were we to cure AIDS.

AIDS is <u>not</u> God's will.

That, however, is like saying cancer, polio, and T.B. are also God's will and we should not be trying to eradicate them, either. But that doesn't make sense. I cannot believe that God intends that we stand around watching passively while our fellow humans suffer and die when we can choose to do otherwise using the intelligence He gave us to attack these disastrous diseases. Rather, it seems to me that God has allowed global and personal tragedy to flourish for reasons other than punishment of those He doesn't favor. I'm inclined to think that He wants humans to strive to overcome these problems, large and small, as we encounter them and grow in the process of doing so. God wants us to advance as individuals, as societies, as religions, and as civilizations. In short, I think He wants us to work alone and together to overcome life's flaws and adversities as we learn from each other and Him. That is a major part of my answer to the "Why me?" question.

We Are Instruments of God

An apt metaphor for God's methods in achieving our spiritual growth is the Israelites' saga presented in the Bible. The story takes place in Mesopotamia, Egypt, and Canaan and it recounts His formation of one nomadic family into a nation that survived and grew down through the ages despite trials that would have destroyed lesser souls. (This is a tale that I will revisit in subsequent chapters.) In the books of Exodus, Numbers, and Deuteronomy we are given a fascinating picture of how God has told us He works. The saga focuses on a whimpering bunch of slaves who were forced to leave their homes and stew pots in one of the cradles of civilization. They fled because they feared they would be blamed for the plagues God had visited on Pharaoh and the people of Egypt, not the least of which was the death of all Egyptian firstborn, including Pharaoh's own son. None of the Israelites wanted to hang around and find out what the consequences would be when their children had been the only ones spared in all the land along the Nile.

To get them out of Egypt, God provided a charismatic human leader in the prophet Moses, parted the Red Sea (or the Sea of Reeds, depending on the English translation of the Bible you favor), led them with pillars of fire by night and smoke by day, provided manna from heaven, and brought forth water from solid rock. Despite all these Divine manifestations that were held up before their very eyes day after day and night after night, the newly-nomadic Israelites still bemoaned their lot. They cursed Moses for leading them away from what they remembered as the good life in the land of Goshen as they forgot that they had been forced to make mud bricks without straw and had been a fearful and trembling rabble. They just wanted to be left alone, without a challenge from God or anyone else.

Ignoring their preferences, God took them to their new home-to-be by the short route and showed them Canaan. Once there, following Moses' instructions, each of the twelve tribes sent a scout into the Promised Land to find out what awaited them in this new country. All of the scouts confirmed that the place did flow with milk and honey, but ten of the twelve told horrific tales of invincible giants inhabiting the place and claimed it couldn't be taken. Two young scouts, Joshua and Caleb, disagreed. They maintained that all those obstacles could be overcome; however, no one among the defeatist Israelites wanted to be the first to try. After much debate, the Israelites, in hang-dog obedience to what they concluded was God's wishes, made a halfhearted attack and got their butts kicked. They had started with a negative, forlorn mindset and couldn't overcome it or the Canaanites.

The Israelites got their butts kicked.

We are told God did what I'm convinced He always does with us humans—He set out to mold the Israelites into what He needed them to be. He turned the twelve tribes around and marched them into the desert for forty years of His version of "boot camp." They learned to march in precise military order and each tribe camped every day in its assigned location around the meeting tent that housed the Ark of the Covenant. Judah, Issachar, and Zebulon always camped to the east; Ruben, Simeon, and Gad to the south; Ephraim, Manasseh, and Benjamin to the west, and Dan, Asher, and Naphtali to the north. On the march and in camp, every man was to be in his proper place within his own division. They assembled, moved, and conducted battle exercises in response to the signals from silver trumpets.

And battle they did, time and time again. If they disobeyed Moses or rebelled, retribution was swift and terrible. Over those forty years, God let the pessimistic, fainthearted slaves that had fled Egypt in fear one jump ahead of Pharaoh die off. In their stead, He raised their progeny, desert-hardened and battle-trained, to be His new Israel—a People who had not known the gods of Egypt, would believe in Him alone, and follow Him without doubt or question. He did this because He needed to take the Promised Land and plant a new people there who would fan the belief in one true God into a flame that would survive for all time.

God molded the Israelites into what He needed them to be.

Of the old generation, none was allowed to cross over into the new land, with the exception of the two scouts, Caleb and Joshua, who became great leaders. Moses wasn't given that privilege; his time had passed. Instead, he was granted the right to see, from atop a mountain, the promise he had dreamed of over those forty years. Moses died there, having fulfilled the purpose God had assigned to him that he had accepted.

I don't think God was punishing Moses or the older Israelites. True, they suffered grave hardships that included hunger, thirst, fear, and even death. I'm sure that at the time they couldn't see or understand more than a glimmer of God's purpose for them, if that. But they seized the opportunity to be the best they were capable of so that succeeding generations could carry out God's plan for Israel.

When those subsequent generations of Israelites began to backslide in their development, adopting the ways and gods of the pagan tribes and nations that surrounded them, God drove them into Babylonian exile where He further refined them through new adversity. From there, He brought a remnant back to Jerusalem and replanted it in the Promised Land to await the Messiah's coming. As part of this, God inculcated in the Israelites a horror of the idol-worshippers who encircled their new home and molded the Israelites into a tight little nation that grew in its belief in Him as the one true God. He used the Israelites who stood apart from non-believers to incubate human understanding of a single Deity. They had to be capable of sustaining this idea no matter what hardships or hate-based oppressions confronted them, and they were. We are taught that this was God's purpose for these people.

God used the Israelites to incubate human understanding of a single Deity.

God has a purpose for us today just as He had one for the ancient Israelites. It is clear to me that God uses life with all its experiences to shape us, individual by individual, generation by generation, and society by society into a better whole as our flowing advance of humanity moves on towards the destination God has chosen for us. He molds us just as he molded the Israelites.

A Lesson Repeated

In considering God's molding process, I'm persuaded that we haven't changed all that much from those who wandered through the desert more than four thousand years ago. Like them, we have challenges God has set before us and can see different miracles all around us. Yet we often cling to old ways of thinking and doing things. We watch systemic starvation, disease-ridden communities, and an overflowing of global pollution that laps at our feet and do little or nothing because it would require personal sacrifice. "It's always been that way so why should we try and change it now. Besides, they're not my neighbors, not my concern so don't ask me to pay a price for them," may be our cry, but in truth it's only an excuse we make to justify the non-action that stymies self-improvement and societal advancement.

I believe God challenges us to change that thinking and tries to mold us into being better than that. We must learn the lessons we're being taught or we will find ourselves wandering for whatever periods in latter-day "deserts" while current generations die off. We can reach our Promised Land if we change ourselves and our behavior toward each other. We must face the fact that life is a challenge to be mastered by each of us individually and as societal composites; it's not something to hide from just because it has its rough parts. The world has plenty of strife that is waiting to be addressed, and every one of us has shortcomings that can be improved, so it is up to us all to leave the world a better place in whatever way we can.

We cling to old ways of thinking and doing things.

We must grasp the concept that God uses life to mold us. He has made it clear to us that He is not there to protect us every moment of every day, especially when that protection would counter His goals for us as individuals or for humanity as a whole. We must recognize that the suffering of some of us should motivate all of us to meet the challenge of that suffering by finding ways to alleviate it. In doing so, we grow. God knows this. He knows that this is what pushes us into inventing new cures or better systems of government, to acts of kindness or heroism. In short, He spurs us on to growth as individuals and societies so that we may better approximate His spirit.

In this light of helping others, one of my personal heroes is a fellow with whom I share a surname but not blood kinship. His name is Jose Pedro Greer. "Joe" is a Cuban-American doctor who has devised new, more effective ways to provide healthcare to the uninsured, the homeless, and the addicted. He crawls under overpasses and viaducts to find them, listens to them, and treats them during his unconventional house calls with methods that are both appreciated and accepted. He hasn't made a lot of money doing this, but he has grown his heart to the point where he can take in the suffering of a never-ending stream of street people without breaking or turning away. He accepts them for who they are with love, a smile, and the humor to make them laugh. Joe and I make media appearances together to beg for money for public radio, to work on homeless issues together, and to break bread with several of our other unrelated namesakes in our "Great Gathering of Greers."

We can reach our Promised Land.

Like Joe, there are those among us who see ills and problems and naturally attack them. Here a disease is conquered, there a system is devised to reduce poverty and someplace else a concept of values is produced that promotes justice. Small kindnesses are bestowed everywhere. Slowly, ever so slowly it seems, we, generation by generation, improve ourselves. Joe Greer has taught me that our awareness of the dark side of life can make us want to overcome that darkness and improve ourselves, our societies, and our world as time goes by.

It's my guess that life will always present problems. Our reward for doing God's work and solving problems is the opportunity to solve more problems, and that is how it should be until there are none left. There is no Valhalla here on Earth, free of all difficulties and challenges. None of us can be an island that is insulated from the rest of humanity. Each of us is woven by Him into a far, far vaster tapestry of purpose. We have to accept reality as seen through God's moral telescope that identifies our unique place in His vast Universe and our individual role in the onward march of humanity as a whole. When we do, we can take up the challenges God gives us.

A representative example of this is the World War II German theologian and minister, Dietrich Bonhoeffer. By all accounts, Bonhoeffer was a very good person and a gifted theologian. At the outbreak of war in 1939, he was in the United States on a lecture tour. Even though he was anti-Nazi, had denounced Hitler on the radio in 1933, and had been banned from Berlin and forbidden to teach in Germany, he forsook the opportunity for asylum in America. Instead, Bonhoeffer returned to Germany to minister to his people. He joined the small, beleaguered resistance movement there and added his efforts to those in opposition to Hitler. This dedicated minister became an influential nuisance and was arrested in early 1943.

The suffering of others should motivate us to action.

Bonhoeffer was imprisoned in various locations, including the Buchenwald Concentration Camp, until he was executed by Gestapo hangmen at Flossenburg Prison in 1945 just before the war's end. In the varied jail cells he had occupied before his demise, he had written an extraordinary amount of material that survived him and it was published after the war as *Letters & Papers From Prison*. Bonhoeffer's writings have had a substantial impact on modern theology and the thoughts of many religious leaders and thinkers. Clearly, God did not punish Dietrich Bonhoeffer for his opposition to tyranny or for his faith. Instead, God used him to influence the rest of us as he became the absolute most he was capable of under the circumstances of his time and place.

With Dietrich Bonhoeffer's life as an example, I feel we must come to understand that God is not simply an unbiased arbiter or referee making the playing field level and fair between individuals, parties, peoples and nations. Just ask Bonhoeffer and the Canaanites about that. They learned that God has an agenda. Life is not innately fair or just; fairness and justice exist only when and where we choose to create them. What God is teaching us, in part through Dietrich Bonhoeffer's writings and the actions of people like Doctor Joe Greer, is that the creation of justice and fairness is among humanity's noblest goals and highest achievements.

The Living Christ

God challenges every one of us to fit into His plan in the way that best helps individuals and humanity grow towards their maximum potential. We can reject that challenge and wallow in our own despair if we want to. Or we can choose to accept them and move His plan forward. There is no better example of this than Christ's life, the establishment of his Church, and the forging of Christianity through time. God used the trial, torture, crucifixion, and death of Jesus of Nazareth—unfair and gruesome things—as the catalytic events that precipitated Christianity out of the Jewish faith. Jesus' followers had been sure that all their hopes for the long-sought Messiah were rotting away with his corpse sealed in a tomb of stone; his subsequent resurrection had unsurpassable power and impact. As a result, their faith in the "new way" he had imparted to them during his ministry on Earth was able to withstand attack by the combined forces of Jewish orthodoxy and Roman secular might.

God forced this new faith outward from Judaism into the world of pagan gentiles. He set Jesus up as a person certain to be rejected by mainstream Jewish society that had been programmed to await a savior in the warrior mold of King David. These ancient Jews saw themselves as the center of the Universe and envisioned a champion who would destroy their enemies and restore their freedom to live in isolated worship of the one true God. They wanted to share their Yahweh with no one because that's the way God had, for several thousand years, taught and molded them to think. And they were true to this God-driven indoctrination. The majority of Jesus' Jewish contemporaries couldn't accept a Jew without pedigree or recognized source of education. Their Messiah couldn't come, they thought, from the despised Galilean backwater of Nazareth. Their savior could not be someone who regularly transgressed the strict tenets and laws of Moses, someone who wasn't focused on expelling the hated gentile Roman overlords, someone who ended up dying the death of one accursed—nailed to a cross.

Fairness and justice exist where we choose to create them.

Jesus teaches us, as he taught the crowds who came to hear him, that "...if you do not eat the flesh of the Son of Man and drink his blood you have no life in you." [John 6:51-58] But entrenched Jewish elders interpreted this as cannibalism and many Jews were shocked by such an implication. Under the dietary laws of Moses, meat had to be drained of blood and under no circumstances was blood to be consumed. To do so was anathema to the devout Jews of Jesus' time, just as it is for those today who keep kosher.

Jesus' teachings horrified the majority of observant Jews who surrounded him. That alone would have caused them to reject any suggestion that he could be their long-awaited Messiah. Clearly, Jesus would have known this, yet he continued to preach about the need to partake of his body. Missing the figurative meaning of his words, Orthodox Jews continued to deny his status and mission. That forced his followers outward from the Israelite nation.

Had God protected Jesus from all harm, as so many of us want to be protected, what would have happened? The Messiah would have lived out his life to a ripe old age, teaching and healing within the small areas of Galilee, Judea, and Jerusalem. Being human, Jesus would have then died a natural death. We would probably be reading today about just another prophet; Jesus would have been the third of a trilogy of prophets, conjoined with Elijah and Elisha. And Christianity would be only a minor Jewish sect based on his teachings.

Jesus' Jewish contemporaries couldn't accept a Jew without pedigree.

Instead, God used terribly unfair and painful events to give birth to, and force outward, His new way from what was at the time a small, insular, and isolated Jewish nation. He used this mechanism to thrust what became Christianity into the surrounding sea of a pagan gentile world. At the same time, God left His Israelites true to the faith and beliefs it had taken Him millennia to instill in them. Both outcomes were part of His plan.

So I would ask us to ask ouselves: If God would not protect His own Son from such hideous earthly harm, but instead used Jesus' life and suffering to advance all of humanity, why should we think He would treat us differently and protect each of us from lesser misfortune?

We shouldn't.

We must grapple with the fact that human life is, at its core, an individual experience. Each of us must live our lives within our own skins and with our own hearts and minds, dealing with our personal bundles of abilities, limitations, fears, hopes, beliefs, and prejudices. It is from this starting point that we reach out to interact with others who define us based on how they perceive our interaction with them. It seems to me that the tendency for most of us, in our individual isolation, is to seek approval, not from ourselves or God, but from other people. And based on what I've seen, far too many of us define approval in terms of the opinions of relative strangers we think of as "them" or "they," or in terms of the money, power, and material goods we amass from other people. We ask what "they" think about me or what "they" will pay me or what "they" will do for me.

Advancing to Decline

The questions above produce excruciating tensions between the fulfillment of inner needs that gives us life and the fulfillment of our supposed needs for material gain and social approval. Such tensions lead to persistent unhappiness; if we want to be happy, I think we must perceive ourselves in terms of the world as it actually is and who we can be.

Moving into the third millennium, masses of humanity are the proud possessors of great wealth. At the same time, there are even larger masses who know nothing but grinding poverty. There are far, far more of us—six billion-plus souls, remember—alive today than have lived in any century of humanity's history. People today are the beneficiaries of technology that was only the stuff of science fiction a mere sixty years ago. Men have gone to the moon and we are reaching out to the very edges of the Universe in search of knowledge. Today's medical sciences have advanced to levels that had only been dreamed about a short time ago. That we can fly through the air and live under water are ho-hum facts now. We have harnessed the awesome forces of the atom and have more computing power at our finger tips than that of all the human beings who ever lived. We have unraveled the human genome and can clone living creatures.

We are "technolized" rather than civilized.

Yet, with all of this, most people, rich or poor, are still filled with disquiet. It appears to me that all across the world our differing societies have certain negative things in common that generate unhappiness: greed, stress, fear of others, spontaneous anger, and collective self-righteousness. In effect, humanity is engulfed by huge amounts of knowledge but little real wisdom. Based on that knowledge, our age thinks of itself as civilized. I suggest we are not. What we haven't mastered is ourselves and the ability to truly care and share with others. Until humanity does that we remain uncivilized, albeit technically proficient, barbarians. Civilization is based on how people deal with each other and the world they share. Technology simply provides the mechanical and material means for doing so. To quote Dr. Martin Luther King, "Our scientific power has outrun our spiritual power. We have guided missiles and misguided men."

I'm convinced that, at best, we are "technolized" rather than civilized and that's a very dangerous situation. Right now, technology and fear of others' use of it controls humanity; we must learn to reverse that process.

We're intelligent enough now as a species to know what it means to be civilized, but we're still a long way from that. If the countless personal transgressions each of us commits aren't proof enough of how primitive we still are, no world that tolerates Rwandas, Bosnias, Cambodian killing fields, slavery, starvation, epidemics in countries that can't afford treatment because effective existing drugs are priced beyond their means for profits' sake, mass illiteracy, gender, race or class discrimination, and religious intolerance could claim to be civilized. Humanity will only be so when we have the wisdom to live our unique lives thinking of and treating each other as equal, and equally human, no matter how different our appearance, wealth, backgrounds, or beliefs might be. To my way of thinking, life is too short for anything else.

Reverse the Trend

Self-mastery is the critical first step to turn things around. To achieve it, we have to stop looking for others to blame for our pain, failures, and unhappiness. For the most part, the cures for those deficits have to be found within ourselves. If all we do is point fingers at others as we wallow in our own despair, we will drown in the blame game no matter how many people, institutions, or systems can rightly be accused of sharing some of the responsibility for our shortcomings. I'm convinced it is crucial for us to embrace the realities of our personal lives in light of our relationships with each other and with God. I'd contend that we're advanced enough intellectually to know that it is long past the time that an overwhelming majority of people should have started looking within for the answers that lead to global civilization.

Modern society has sold too many of us on the myth that we are entitled to live in a perfect world, pain-free and unchallenged. We want to be oblivious to anything but our own pleasure and contentment. Our inner voice, however, tells us how wrong such striving is as we continue down that same path. Every material gain only serves to reinforce the truth that nothing tangible can fill the void we all have. The truth is that life contains differing measures of happiness, heartache, and the unexpected that are, for better or for worse, the crucibles of our growth. If we embrace our challenges and choose to go in a different direction that helps others, we will get to that unity under God where everyone will be, as Bonhoeffer was, the most that they can be.

It's long past the time that the majority of people should have started looking within for answers.

While happiness is truly to be sought after, it is folly for us to think we are entitled to pass our lives in bliss, exempt from the sacrifices that are necessary for any creditable endeavor. As Queen Elizabeth II said in a letter to New York City and the world soon after 9/11, "Grief is the price we pay for love." Anything worth doing and any relationship worthy of pursuit have pain and sacrifice on some level that go along with happiness and personal reward. They are twinned pairs, dualities that bind a life worth living together. Let us embrace them; we owe it to ourselves, our world and generations yet to come not to flee from life's experiences or the vast diversity that surrounds us. Because it is how we deal with those experiences that can shape a better future.

In a significant way, each of us is a unique individual who is responsible in part for the overall human condition. We can speak about our selfish interests, or listen to the truth of the ages. We can perish alone, or survive together. The challenge is to find our way by finding ourselves in others. All of us must conduct our lives as God intends us to, ever mindful of the striving of each of us. We should be thinking about how our own trials can be offered up for the benefit of others. That's how both God's plan and the best possible future will be realized.

We are insignificant unless we see the significance in everyone else.

Each of us has to come to grips with the fact that God loves us, but, just as Galileo discovered with celestial bodies, we cannot be the center of God's existence or focus; it's the other way around. So what does God want from us? Humility. Acknowledgment that we are insignificant unless we see significance in everyone else. Understanding that our reason for being is to focus on the oneness God is pushing us towards. As inconsequential as we may be on the grandest scale, each of us can make the sphere that is close by better.

Those who choose not to believe would declare that God is a myth and there is no grand plan. For them there is no hope of protection from harm and discomfort, and from humans wreaking evil on other humans, because God doesn't step in. Ergo, there can be no God. They'll add that as we humans with all our modern scientific knowledge and analytical skills cannot identify and quantify God, detect His presence through scientific proof, or explain His origin, He does not exist.

I beg to differ. He does exist, and we exist for Him.

TWO
Follow, or Lead—Discerning the Truth

G od molds us and I believe that from time to time over the millennia, He has inspired a series of laws meant to direct our thinking and conduct. These ordinances have an inescapable logic to them based on the issues that they were intended to address. However, to fully understand that logic as well as its current applicability, it has occurred to me that we must consider the needs, knowledge, and conditions that surrounded the human drafters of those laws.

Historically, people have written about and striven to understand God, what He would have us do, and life itself in terms, symbols, and concepts they could understand. Without that context, nothing would have had meaning to them. Such understanding was restricted by the scope of human knowledge available to those writers and their societies, just as ours is limited by the sum of human understanding available to us today.

For example, as a new nation with a very narrow world view and minimal scientific information, the Israelites were given a complex and complete code of laws that addressed property rights, inheritance, morality, purity, and customs such as dietary restrictions and circumcision. The Israelites felt compelled to follow those laws to the letter and attempted to rigidly adhere to each and every one of them. The law was simply there to be obeyed, no questions asked. Today, many of us ignore the context of the difficulties and issues those people faced at that time and remain rigid in observance of the same ancient code.

Many of us remain rigid in observance of an ancient code.

When we view God's laws in the context of the period when they were set down, we can see what He was trying to accomplish with the Israelites: improvement and preservation of a threatened society. God's starting point in this effort was, as it always is, love, and He implements that love by inspiring rules for conduct. We humans, on the other hand, tend to look at the rules first and work backwards from there to the realization of God's love. Thus, the rules often become more important than the love that engendered them. If, however, we consider God's ordinances in light of the circumstances in which they were written and find that early rules no longer accomplish their God-set goals, I believe God allows them to be changed.

For example, consider the "laws" that deal with human procreation. Many people read the Bible and believe that God has set down a hard and fast rule that a man "shall not spill his seed on the ground." There is no such ordinance; there is, however, the tale of Onan in Genesis 38. According to this Biblical story, God punished Onan with death when he disobeyed his father, Judah, and refused to impregnate his widowed sister-in-law. Onan chose to spill his seed on the ground rather than raise children in his dead brother's name and line.

Some of the faithful have inferred from Onan's story the above-mentioned "rule." That has become the basis for the argument now that the limitation of the Earth's population through birth control is evil and against the will of God. But when that story was told, the world was a far different place than it is today. In those ancient days, God was focused on ensuring the survival of a nomadic clan that He was building into the nation of Israel. Their numbers had to be increased to a level where they could conquer the Promised Land. The world was grossly under-populated with humans whose lives were short, brutish, and dangerous. Thus, there was clear logic to God's intent and desire for the Israelites in particular and mankind in general to multiply.

God allows us to change some of His laws.

Today, however, that logic no longer holds true. Our world is overpopulated in many areas where capacities are being strained to their very limit in support of ever-increasing numbers. This overpopulation can and does threaten humanity's survival in the future. But it won't, if we use our God-given brains and reasoning based on the modern knowledge we have to modify this "rule," control our numbers, and survive in our present circumstances.

The question for me then becomes: Does God still want us to follow a law given to save us long ago, when that same law might do the opposite and destroy us today? It is illogical to think that God would ask us to enforce an ordinance that threatens the very existence of what I believe God wishes to preserve—humankind. I cannot believe that God wishes us to be lemmings, hurling ourselves toward destruction just because we cannot conceive, no matter what the modern circumstances might be, that He would allow one of the laws He inspired in imperfect subjects millennia ago to be changed or modified today.

Thinking about that reminded me of growing up in Alexandria, Virginia, in the late nineteen-forties. My father had a friend, an inveterate practical joker who always played tricks on those around him. People had grown tired of his pranks and wanted to let him know that they were no longer funny. At that time, the state of Virginia had a number of laws dating from the early seventeen-hundreds still on its statute books. Under one of these ordinances, if one-hundred property owners got up a petition, they could have a man hung by the local magistrate. So, not only did Dad and ninety-eight other men prepare and sign such a petition, they also duped the jokester into signing it as the hundredth name to approve of his own hanging!

Laws must have an ongoing reason that serves the needs of those governed.

Needless to say, that sentence was never carried out. I hope the joker got the message. Sometime thereafter, Virginia purged its statues of such anachronisms. Even if long ago there had been sound purposes and a need for such a statute, one can no longer have someone executed through the mechanism of a landholders' petition.

More recently, the State of Massachusetts repealed an archaic law dating from 1675 that prohibited American Indians from setting foot within the City of Boston. It had been passed at a time when the Massachusetts Bay Colony was at war with the surrounding Indian tribes. The Puritans in the Colony vilified Indians as heathen savages as the two groups fought over lands in the Colony's pathways for expansion. At the start of the twenty-first century, that law was still on the statute books and was nothing but a meaningless regulation. So it was repealed and now Native Americans can freely enter the City of Boston without fear of breaking the law.

To be valid, rules and laws must have an ongoing reason that serves the needs of those governed. All too often in our history, we have created regulations for good and proper reasons and then those reasons disappeared but the rules live on, just like Virginia's old hanging law and Massachusetts' anti-Indian statute. Likewise, the first lawgiver, God, inspired the men and women who wrote the books of the Bible to lay down certain rules for human conduct. Those ordinances were good and proper based on mankind's needs at the time. But we must remind ourselves that drafters of those laws were limited by the exigencies of their surroundings, their understanding of the world they lived in, and the body of human knowledge then. The majority of these ordinances remain absolutely valid today because the human condition has not changed all that much. But that is not true with all of them.

Laws Are Meant to be Changed

I think it is up to us to reexamine ancient rules in the light of God's clear logic and purpose in calling them forth. We must determine whether the same regulations would be promulgated if God were inspiring the Bible today. In that light, we might find that, based on His love for us, He would allow some of the old ordinances to be changed.

In fact, God has done this at times. All you have to do is hold the Old Testament up against the New. When you do that, it becomes quite apparent that Jesus was a breaker of God's original rules. Time and time again, he disregarded God's old laws and, on behalf of God, gave us new ones. In fact, Jesus' way became known as the "new way" of God. Let us not forget that when Jesus encountered laws that were no longer appropriate or created loads too heavy for humanity to bear, he broke those laws. God so loved mankind that He sent His son Jesus to teach us, among other things, how to break them, how to change them ourselves when it is necessary.

God sent His son Jesus to teach us how to break laws.

The most glaring examples concerned the Sabbath laws. The old rule was that you could not work on the Sabbath, no matter what the urgency was. Jesus showed us that working on God's holy day is allowed if it helps or saves other human beings. Jesus broke the old rules in favor of new and better ones that met the needs of his day. Consider, too, Jesus' command to call no one here on Earth "Father," found in Matthew 23:1-10. Jesus was referring to teachers, rabbis, and, by extension, priests. He wanted us to think for ourselves as we serve each other. Yet we have no trouble calling people "Father" today without worrying about Biblical admonitions.

A more compelling example is slavery. We are taught that God approved of it under certain conditions. He said to Moses: "Slaves, male and female, you may indeed possess." [Leviticus 25:44-46] In Exodus 21, He gave us laws governing how those slaves were to be treated. Today, we have changed those rules by outlawing the practice of one human owning another. In the U.S., we fought a terrible civil war to abolish slavery and I hope no one would ever suggest we go back to it. Likewise, I cannot believe that any religious person thinks slavery is an institution God approves as it is contrary to the well-being of humanity.

Of course, humans aren't perfect and we often make new rules that don't conform to His intent. We are motivated by expediency and after some time has passed, we act as if the new directive was always there to be obeyed by all. However, when our efforts are misguided, God lets us know about that sooner or later. The modern-day Catholic Church's difficulties in staffing its priesthood of "fathers" might be an illustrative example.

When our efforts are misguided, God will let us know.

The apostles, as well as the early Church's bishops and deacons, had been allowed to marry even though they filled priest-like offices. But the Church changed the rules later on, demanding that priests and bishops be celibate because it felt that was necessary for the well-being of the Church and, by extension, all of humanity. (The Church's financial security vis-à-vis inheritance no doubt influenced its reasoning in setting the standard of celibacy.)

We should keep in mind Jesus' words that warn us against "making dogmas out of human precepts." [Matthew 15:3-9] Instead, I believe what he wanted us to learn is how to love and serve each other in light of the world we confront, not the world of ages gone by. The Church is learning with ever-increasing clarity the price it is paying to maintain its rule of celibacy for clerics in a society where a priest is called "Father," despite Christ's advice, but isn't allowed to fulfill that office in its most cherished human purpose. It may now be time for the Catholic Church to reexamine this rule to better serve the people it is meant to help.

It may now be time for the Catholic Church to reexamine celibacy.

Another great religious teacher of modern times has reminded us of the need for human reexamination. I understand that in his thoughts on the just-passed millennium, the Dalai Lama told people to "open your arms to change, but don't let go of your values." He is also attributed with: "Learn the rules so you know how to break them properly." We often forget these lessons, to our detriment. We fall into the trap of thinking like modern-day scribes and Pharisees. Like many of them, we seem incapable of the reevaluation required to meet humanity's real and current needs—God's purpose for us that is based on His love. I wonder why that is so. It may be because our attention and vision is fixed to the rear; we humans are fascinated with history and how things used to be done. We travel to museums and ruins, look up our individual genealogies, and study the lessons of the past. I think we do that because we can see the past and know its outcome when the future is shrouded in uncertainty.

A Different Perspective

Efforts at historic understanding are invaluable and teach us much that we need to know. This fascination, however, can keep us from thinking about the future beyond our own lifetimes or those of our children and grandchildren. This often myopic focus on the lessons of history can sometimes drag us into a closed loop. It prevents us from making the breakthroughs we need to achieve to advance into the future God has in mind for us. Pope Urban's refusal to look at Galileo's new scientific proofs is a perfect example of this. Like Urban, we drift on the river of time looking only backward to where that river has come from and at the river traffic we are traveling with. We do not give much thought to where time's river leads beyond the horizon of our individual lives. This is understandable because we believe we will only travel a minute part of that river's unimaginable length and never reach its ultimate destination. We leave that destination to God or chance according to our beliefs, forgetting that we are all part of an ever-onward-flowing whole for which we are, in some very critical ways, responsible. When we do this, I feel we lose a very important perspective as to where mankind currently is in that river of time and where we are going in our evolution towards our ultimate destiny.

Let's assume the human species is no more than two million years old and that our Earth and Sun can support us in our evolution for another four billion years or so until the Sun, having burned up its hydrogen fuel, expands into an unstable red giant and burns the Earth to a cinder. Some fascinating perspectives emerge with these assumptions.

First, it is clear that humanity's journey has barely begun. In fact, if you compare our two-million-year history with the four billion years we have potentially yet to go, we have completed only one-twentieth of one percent of the trip. Another way to look at it is, if we assume an average life span for individuals in the future of one hundred years, it will take one-hundred-sixty million generational lifetimes laid end to end to reach the end of humanity's evolutionary journey.

Humanity's journey has barely begun.

Given human abilities today, when we are only in our evolutionary infancy, and the developmental possibilities open to us in that vast generational future that lies before us, there is almost no limit to what mankind can choose to become under God's guidance. Yet, even with this promise, we still duck the challenges that God has surrounded us with and I wondered why until I saw the top-grossing movies of recent years. The answer hit me right between the eyes: Superheroes. We look for champions or wizards to appear suddenly and make everything alright for us. It doesn't matter who, as long as someone else comes along and does the dirty work. We'll take God or whomever, just as long as it's not us. We want disease, drug abuse, crime, environmental disasters, and all the other dangers of the world to go away while all we have to do is watch and applaud. We accept all the injustices, disease, and poverty that surround us as long as they don't engulf our personal lives or families. The Holocaust was but one of thousands of examples of what detachment leads to, examples that seem to be with us always, such as today's genocide in Darfur.

Well, superheroes don't exist outside of Hollywood's imagination. None of them is going to leap off of the silver screen and save the day. There *are* heroes among us, but they can't save humanity while the rest of us elect to sit passively by and just watch. It is only by all of us getting involved, choosing to confront the hard, dirty jobs, and taking risks—just as the Israelites did—that we can defeat the ever-increasing dangers we face. It is only when we individually and collectively make positive changes in our lives and societies that the true super-heroic improvements in humanity's condition can occur. No caped crusaders or Hogwarts graduates are going to do that for us.

There <u>are</u> heroes among us.

God won't do all of it for us, either. In His own way, He'll show us how and what to do, but I'm certain the doing must be ours. I'm convinced that we must, all of us, forget our "not-my-job" attitudes and fulfill the potential we have to overcome whatever we face. It is up to those of us living today to create a better tomorrow. We have to make sure that we don't end everything in humanity's infancy with world-destroying forces or pollution, power-obsessed greed, or hidebound conformity to laws—secular or otherwise. Humanity's needs require the best we can give, and rule-breaking is a part of that. We have the power to effect personal and global change. And we must do so. Each of us must do his or her part, take the risks heroes take.

What Would God Have Us Do?

There are examples in the Bible of God actually speaking to the patriarchs and prophets. We are told He pronounced on a mountaintop His pleasure in Jesus within the hearing of three of the Disciples. The prophet Amos, a lowly shepherd from Tekoa in Judah, proclaimed, "The lion roars—who will not be afraid! The Lord God speaks—who will not prophesy!" [Amos 3:8] But God spoke aloud to only a few who abandoned all else to do His bidding and acted as His messengers to humanity. That was true even when kings, priests, and contemporaries hated them for it and even killed them if they did not desist.

In this light, I've heard skeptics ask, if God spoke to humans then, why doesn't He speak out loud to us in the here and now? If God wants His laws changed, why doesn't He just do it Himself? It sure would make life a lot easier and would prove that God does, indeed, exist. But I believe it's we who must prove ourselves to God, not the other way around.

God wants us to choose to be more like Him.

Were God to speak to us directly now as we are told He did long ago, He would direct our conduct and give us our laws. We would rely on Him to think for us instead of thinking for ourselves. We would be frozen in place like a herd of flawed cattle, contentedly grazing where and on what He told us to, forever the same. But that is not God's purpose for us. God wants us to exercise our own free will in dealing with individual and world problems. He wants us to choose to be more like Him. By wrestling with the problems of society and faith and choosing the best laws and doing what is right without God's open intervention, we improve on our own, we grow and mature in His garden. It seems to me that God has stepped back because He doesn't want His voice to interfere with humanity's growth. He spoke just enough to get us on the right track, knowing it is the act of overcoming problems that forces individuals and humanity to improve.

When I think about this I am reminded of a humorous tale I have heard off and on most of my life. It seems the daughter of a hard-line Southern preacher stumbled across her father slumped drunkenly against a tree behind one of the local roadhouses just outside of their little town. Apparently, a few of the good old boys in their congregation had been sneaking whiskey out the back to him because he couldn't be seen drinking inside, or anywhere else for that matter. Shaking her head in dismay, the girl cried, "Papa, Papa, what would God say if He saw you like this?" Looking up with bleary eyes at his daughter, the preacher replied in a slurred voice, "He does child, he does. He just keeps what he thinks to himself—and so should you."

We are responsible for a better future.

Like the preacher, endowed as we are with the free will to choose, we elect to block God out and not listen to Him when he does, in fact, speak to us through our hearts and souls, or we choose to just disbelieve entirely. To me, this is a big reason God became man in Jesus Christ. In human form, He could speak with, preach to and teach us directly without overwhelming us or co-opting our free will. Without absolute control from on high, God wants us to make our own choices to act morally as we solve our problems and meet life's crises. If we choose to use the gift of free will wisely, we will prosper. If not, we will perish—and I don't think that's what a loving God wants for us at all.

But we are a stubborn bunch. God is interested in substance over form, and yet mankind proves time after time that we are focused on form over substance. We want people and societies to adhere to the letter of the law no matter how ridiculous an outcome that adherence produces. God, on the other hand, cares more about the concrete results we are achieving through His universal laws. This difference is something the prophets and psalmists have pointed out to us time and time again on God's behalf. As any number of them has said, it is not our burnt offerings that God wants; He wants our love for one another and for Him.

God's repeated desire for us is that we deal honestly and kindly with each other, do that which is right and just. I don't think He cares much about quaint formalities of worship or the nature of our public offerings. Instead, I would argue that it is we who need to listen to God's voice, as in Psalms 50: 7-15:

Hear, my people, and I will speak; Israel, I will testify against you; God, your God, am I.

Not for your sacrifices do I rebuke you, for your holocausts are before me always.

I take from your house no bullock, no goats out of your fold.

For mine are all the animals of the forests, beasts by the thousands on my mountains.

I know all the birds of the air, and whatever stirs in the plains belongs to me.

If I were hungry, I should not tell you, for mine are the world and its fullness.

Do I eat the flesh of strong bulls, or is the blood of goats my drink?

Offer to God praise as your sacrifice and fulfill your vows to the Most High;

Then call upon me in times of distress; I will rescue you, and you shall glorify me.

This message is repeated in one form or another throughout the Bible and the rest of the world's sacred writings. But many of us do not want to hear God's words in this regard. Instead, human history demonstrates that we remain steadfastly obsessed with the form and formalities we have created for our worship of Him, no matter what our faith is, while we brutalize and debase the substance of His teachings and intent.

What We Do Instead

Like the preacher in the joke who drank himself into a stupor, we want to tell people to do as we say, not as we do. We want to be seen, not by God, but by our fellow humans at church, temple, or mosque on Sabbaths and Holy Days as we supposedly worship God. Too often, we learn nothing from God while we are there because we are too busy telling Him our troubles and how things ought to be. We demand He follow our instructions in setting them right. All the while, we blithely go on dehumanizing and killing one another in battles resulting from interpretations of the Trinity, or disagreements about the correct way to worship God, or about what the true faith is. We totally ignore His message that transcends religion to love all mankind and refrain from harming one another.

I have observed that, immersed as we are in vanity, we often either disclaim God altogether or are tempted to think we can cajole, coerce, bargain with, or bribe God into doing what we want as opposed to doing what God has planned for us. How often have we told God that if He will only take away a current tribulation, we will be good and follow His ways at last? We threaten that if He doesn't do what we want, we will stop believing in Him. When God's decisions don't conform to our expectations, we declare God dead or nonexistent, turn our backs, and even try to take others with us as we deny His presence.

Some of us flatter ourselves by thinking that we are in control and that God needs our adulation and worship. But I cannot believe God craves our adoration. Instead, it is we who need and long for God in our lives on a daily basis, whether or not we are aware of it. If we are frank with ourselves, we will concede that it is we who want Him to walk constantly at our sides. I'm persuaded that we must put our relationship with God into its proper prospective. He is God and we are His servants. He loves us, but will nonetheless use us for His purposes, notwithstanding our vain pretensions and insistent wants.

We must put our relationship with God into its proper perspective.

Despite this truth that has been drummed into us for all time, many of us feel that we should not stoop in humility and quietly petition God for help on a daily basis or in times of distress. We are too proud and in our pride we, whether we recognize it or not, see ourselves as having attributes approaching those of God. In our minds, we are within shouting distance of being His equal. And, as I have been told, one does not beg from an equal. So, instead, we bellow commands to Him like spoiled children. When we refuse to ask for God's help, we are effectively spurning it even as it is being offered, albeit in a different way than expected. If we don't see that, we are only hurting ourselves. We don't prove that we are God's near equals when we offer Him "gifts" from our holdings as a bargain in exchange for His blessings. We show how little we respect Him when we reject calling His name after our proffered worldly goods do not seem to move Him.

It has been suggested that we need to learn once and for all that nothing physical or material in our possession is ours forever. Ownership is fleeting; possessions are something God has given to us to use for a finite time. Sooner or later, we must pass them on to be used by someone else. That individual, in turn, has to leave them to yet another in a never-ending cycle.

Ownership is fleeting.

The only things in this world we have that are ultimately and uniquely our own are our individual lives and souls and the character we choose to infuse into them. What we need to be building foremost in this life is not material wealth, but the personal relationships that multiply with loving interaction with God and those around us, near and far. Our growth should be based on the simple basic rules He has laid down for us that are centered on consideration, empathy, and fair dealing. I trust God will judge us on how hard we try to do that, not on how much wealth we have accumulated or how much regard strangers have for us. Those things are only poor, shabby substitutes for what really matters.

The hubris of humanity in believing otherwise is reflected over and over again in the Bible's stories. Consider, for example, the Israelites' fall from grace after God led them to the Promised Land. Despite all they had been through and everything God had taught them and done for them, the Israelites were more concerned with acceptance by the peoples that surrounded them than they were with God's message and approval. They wanted to be like the Philistines, Canaanites, and Egyptians. They were afraid of being different from, and having to face the disapproval of, other nations and peoples. Because everyone else had hereditary kings, the Israelites wanted their own. The judges God had bestowed on them just weren't good enough.

God should be served with humility and selflessness.

Other peoples' gods were represented by tangible graven images, so the Israelites wanted the same, even though God had explicitly forbidden them. When the worshipers of false gods came into their nation as wives, slaves, or traders, the Israelites began to think they should hedge their bets and pay homage to Baal and the wooden images that accompanied the outsiders. Some of the Israelites even adopted horrific sacrificial practices, such as burning alive their own children, because others worshipped their gods that way. As yet another example of how God makes us pay for such acts that abrogate the rules He wishes to remain in force, He brought about the defeat, degradation, and exile of the Jews from the Promised Land to renew His teachings about false idols and about how the one God should be served with humility and selflessness, with love of others as one loves himself.

Today, many folks still believe as the Israelites did that God punished them because their formalistic rituals weren't perfect enough, their altar sacrifices were insufficient to please Him. Such shallow understanding of true worship is but another of the many examples that value form over substance. Whenever we do that, God disciplines us the way small children are disciplined—first with reason, then with coercion. Rather than meting out gratuitous punishment, God was teaching the Israelites and all who came after them the difference between obedience and rebellion and between right and wrong. History has demonstrated that His comeuppances have advanced and civilized people who paid a dear price—suffering and death—for vain worship.

So, again, what should our relationship with God be? What should we be saying to the Lord and how should we be saying it? What should we do to worship Him? Certainly, it cannot be based on our whining, petulance, and vanity. We can, however, strive to understand Him better and serve Him better by giving ourselves up to Him. We worship God by living daily as He would have us live—doing unto others as we would have them do unto us. We also worship God when we commune with Him through prayer when we feel the need for His guidance and counsel, or when we have cause to be thankful. This is the kind of worship that has meaning.

Hear His Voice

I am convinced God does speak to us in his own way and that the majority of time it isn't in the form of punishment via pestilence and war. Most of the time, He speaks more subtly via the millions of miraculous kindnesses that occur every day between and among people. They might not be readily apparent, but they register in our hearts nonetheless. And when we look at something important in a different way, have an inspiring thought, or turn in a different direction and wonder why, I feel God is speaking to us in his non-auditory way then, too. We just have to listen better. And trust that God will always help, though we may not know how or when He will do so.

What we should always know is that we have to do our part to be saved, from an immediate burden or crisis, or for all eternity. It's like the apocryphal story of the man who had everything and suddenly it all fell apart: His business partners quit on him, took all the company's customers, and left him to cover the expensive lease on their offices; his wife announced she wanted a divorce to marry her personal trainer and, by the way, she wanted big bucks he no longer had; his daughter wrote to say she'd just been admitted to the most expensive medical school in the land, so would he please send a check; the last straw came with a phone call from his son's therapist who informed the man that the kid suffered from an acute lack of self esteem that had resulted from his dad's arrivals at Little League games that had been always just in time to see the boy strike out in the ninth inning as he looked over his shoulder to see if his father was in the stands—therapy was going to cost another bundle.

Real worship occurs outside a church, synagogue, or mosque.

This guy goes to church that afternoon and falls to his knees. "Lord, I've always tried to follow your commands," he prays. "I've given to the poor and I'm kind to my neighbor. But now I need your help. My only hope is to win the lottery." A week goes by and nothing. So he goes back to church and begs out loud, "God, you've got to save me. Please let me win the lottery." Still nothing, so for a third week he sneaks into the empty sanctuary and screams, "Dear God, I'm desperate—the lottery's my last chance. Help me!" Suddenly, the man's heart is filled with a voice that responds, "Listen, fellow, meet me halfway—buy a ticket!'

Too many of us fail to do our parts in our relations with God. We haven't bought a ticket, so to speak, let alone met Him halfway. Simply going to our various churches, temples, and mosques on a regular basis and then cheerfully ignoring God's teachings in between isn't doing our part. Mosques, temples, and churches are where God's values might be preached, but the real worship occurs outside their walls and the challenge is to put our vanity to rest and put what we have heard into practice.

All too often, it seems we have to learn God's lessons the hard way. Even when God does speak to us today in the manner of His choosing, history tells us many don't hear Him or decide not to listen. Stubborn as we are in our free will choices, the only thing we can expect is more hard lessons because we just aren't doing what we're supposed to be doing.

The good news is more of us are choosing to do the right thing

As we keep running into dead ends, the good news is more and more of us are heeding God's message and choosing to do the right thing to change the way things are. More of us are opting to be governed under the highest laws. More of us have faith that individual choices can advance the collective. And when enough of us discern the true meaning of His purpose and follow it, we will be much farther along on the road that leads to the fulfillment of God's plan for us. So, as Isaac Bashevis Singer said, "We have to believe in free will. We've got no choice."

The challenge we face is to find and accept the truth that moves all of us closer to God. He doesn't tap a shoulder and whisper in an ear because He wants each of us to act with faith in His existence, with hope for a better world, and with the love that can make such a world a reality.

THREE
Heed Labels, or Ignore Them—
Mastering Your Flaws

F acing our own prejudices is part of the discovery process. One that many of us have is Anti-Semitism. More than any other group, Jews probably hold the record for being despised by other peoples over the longest period of history. Anti-Semitism, hatred of Jews, has existed for millennia and persists today during our still-unenlightened times. Why is that? Why, of all the world's religions and races, do the Jews invoke such enmity?

We are taught that the Israelites, Jewish predecessors, were blessed as God's Chosen People. We pore over their history in the Bible during Sunday school and church. We know about their forced migration throughout time that resulted from persecution and we marvel at their resiliency and steadfastness that remain to this day. We marvel, too, at their accomplishments in the arts, sciences, business, letters and theology, even as we envy their accomplishments and the wealth some have accumulated. But they, like us, are not perfect. They are only humans who can be identified with ease as members of a distinct clan and non-Jews are often outraged by what they deem to be Jewish clan-wide imperfections. Cursing these perceived failings, much of humanity has punished them or stood by and watched their ostracism, degradation and persecution.

Anti-Semitic early Christians blamed the Jews for not accepting Christ. Much later, Jews were punished for not adopting the teachings of the Prophet Mohammed who, according to Islamic belief, had accepted much of what God had taught the Jews and had spoken for that same God. Now, out of what is clearly envy, the Jew-haters among us punish them for being successful, rich, or talented, and for not sharing their overall bounty in a preferred manner and degree. They ignore the fact that none of us is perfect. We have to ask ourselves, who among us has adequately accepted Christ or followed Mohammed's teachings without error? How can one demand of Jews that which is lacking in oneself?

None of us is perfect.

I was brought face to face with this prejudice and a personal shortcoming in high school. When my family first moved to Miami in the summer of 1953, I made friends with a Jewish kid and palled around with him through ninth grade. My father died the next summer and my mother, sister, and I moved back to Arkansas to be near our extended family. But because my mom couldn't make enough of a living to support us there, we returned to Miami after only one year.

When we did, I went back to the same high school I'd been in and got right back into the swing of things, including being elected to one of the school's prestigious service clubs. I was approached by my Jewish friend from ninth grade who really wanted, you might even say needed, to be accepted by that group. Upon testing the waters, I discovered that the club's members would never elect a Jew, at least that Jew, to their number. So, instead of doing the right thing and making an issue of it, I shrugged my shoulders at my friend in an embarrassed sort of way and fobbed off his inquires rather than buck the establishment I, too, wanted to be accepted by. I've always been ashamed of that. More than fifty years later, I am also ashamed to say that I can no longer remember his name. But the mental picture I have of him as I walked away from his request is as clear as the day it happened and it has bothered me ever since.

Who Killed Christ?

The most illogical form of covert or overt aversion to Jews is based on the suggestion that Jews murdered Christ as a group. For millennia, people have tried to justify their anger at Jewish imperfection based on this idea. Therefore, the argument goes, Christians are entitled to hate and persecute the descendants of their Messiah's supposed killers, and other gentiles are free to get on board as well.

Based on this rationale, it seems to me that we should despise and persecute the Italians, too. Their ancestors who can be traced back to Pontius Pilate and his Roman soldiers were equally involved and perhaps more to blame for Jesus' death. Pilate, in fact, did the dirty work. He carried out the demand for Jesus' execution from the Sanhedrin, the Jewish judicial elite.

At least the Sanhedrin believed Jesus guilty of blasphemy against God. Pilate knew Jesus was either an innocent man or, at worst, a religious revolutionary with a minor following. Pilate could have saved him with just a wave of his hand had he wanted to. Instead, he washed those hands. But that didn't erase his ethnicity; not then, not now. Likewise, we would also have to look to Rome's Legions as well. They were the instrument of control in Judea, just as they were in Rome. It was soldiers from these Legions who actually carried out Pilate's sentence of death after first mocking and then scourging Jesus. They would transmit their own share of guilt to their nation's descendants.

Therefore, if ancestral blame is a valid indictment, Pilate and the descendants of his Roman nationality should share it, too. If we hate today's Jews as the descendants of the killers of Christ, we must also hate the Italians for the same reason. In fact, less than fifty years after their execution of Jesus, the ancestors of modern-day Italians tried to stamp out Christianity by executing two more Jews, Saints Peter and Paul, along with as many of Jesus' followers as they could get their hands on. And, it just so happens that in the Roman armies of Jesus' time you would find ancestors of today's Germans, Frenchmen, Britons, Greeks, and Spaniards in addition to Italians, along with most of the rest of the nationalities that now occupy Europe, North Africa and the Middle East. Thus, we mustn't forget all the genetic descendants of Christ's murderers. It would seem an awful lot of us have his blood on our hands.

An awful lot of us have Christ's blood on our hands.

But we don't hate or persecute Italians or any of those other groups based on a speck of genetic material that could be traced to a handful of forbears who officiated at Calvary. Why? Because we all know it is ridiculous to blame modern-day Italians for what a few proto-Italians did almost two thousand years ago. It follows, then, that it is equally ridiculous to hate the totality of today's Jews for what a small clique of their religious ancestors did two thousand years in the past. It's just an excuse that is used to camouflage one's own shortcomings in the eyes of God, one's role in Christ's execution long ago and in the one he now undergoes every day around our world wherever and whenever hate overpowers love.

Rather than hating the Jews, I think we should honor them. They were the necessary catalyst for two of the world's great belief systems: Christianity and Islam. Without Judaism, neither of these faiths would have come into existence as we know them today and perhaps billions of people would still be waiting to be introduced to God.

God Works in Strange Ways

As I've mentioned, God spent thousands of years focusing the Jews inward on themselves and on the concept that there is only one true God. As part of this process, He twice allowed the Israelite nation to be conquered: first by the Babylonians, leading to Jewish exile to Babylon that began in 597 BCE, and then by the Romans with their total destruction of Jerusalem and its Temple in 70 CE. Those events led to the scattering of Jewish communities across the Middle East and beyond in a Diaspora as the Jews honed what was used later on in the Koran and the New Testament.

God returned an aristocratic remnant of this first Diaspora to the Holy Land to set the stage for the coming of the man from Galilee. Surely He knew that anyone from such a suspect place as Nazareth would have been an unacceptable Messiah to the mainstream Jews of that time. A Galilean's association with that region's gentile and Samaritan populations, combined with his corrupt dialect and harsh accent, would automatically bar him in their eyes from the office of Redeemer.

Jesus, in turn, deliberately played on this conditioning as he courted his countrymen's rejection. He flaunted Mosaic Law and other Jewish traditions. For example, he taught that no food was inherently unclean no matter what the Law said and laughed at the hypocrisy of cleansing food and washing only the exterior of people when it was their inner beings that were contaminated. He regularly and intentionally violated the work ban on the Sabbath by engaging in miraculous healings on the holy day of rest.

Jesus courted his countrymen's rejection.

When Jesus instituted at the Last Supper what later became the Christian Eucharist, he enjoined his followers to think of the bread and wine as his body and blood that they were eating and drinking. Without a doubt, he knew that for pious Jews, the drinking of blood was anathema and the eating of a human body was equally abhorrent as cannibalistic. Both would cause the overwhelming majority of Jews to turn away from him. To the further horror of the Pharisees, Jesus consorted with sinners and excoriated the formal Jewish leadership as represented by the Sanhedrin. In sum, he did everything he could to force Jewish denial of his mission and Divinity.

All of the above and more was done to ensure, both before and after his crucifixion, that Christ's xenophobic countrymen would absolutely not accept him as what they understood to be the promised Messiah. Because of this, his disciples were compelled to turn outward from the Jewish community into the gentile world and propagate their new faith in that direction.

I believe God wanted Jesus and his disciples to be rejected by the Jewish mainstream. After millennia of isolation, an anti-pagan mindset, and a belief in one true God that had been vital for their survival, unbowed or absorbed by larger gentile nations that surrounded them, Jews were understandably wary of outside contact and influences. Even if they had recognized Jesus as the Messiah, their isolationist thinking would have made them incapable of sharing their longed-for savior with the gentile world God had taught them to abhor. But Christ's rejection was not the Jews' fault. That and the subsequent fanning-out of Jews who didn't have a nation into a Diaspora were part of God's plan.

Jews were understandably wary of outside contact and influences.

Jewish communities throughout the Roman world and the rest of the Middle East were indispensable for the propagation of Christianity everywhere. They were a nucleus later on for the development of churches that took root despite rejection by local Jewish majorities. From these scattered communities came the core of Christians who were already steeped in the Jewish tradition of belief in one true God and His teachings as found in the Talmud and Torah. This small core of Judeo-Christians was able to function as the sustaining and teaching base on which God could graft the greater mass of gentile Christians until that mass self-perpetuated. The fact that both religions survive to this day means that God must still want it that way.

Had the Jews not rejected Christ as the Messiah with its consequent forcing of his followers outward from the Jewish nation, the Christian message would in all likelihood have remained locked within the confines of a narrow community. The xenophobia God had pounded into the Israelites would have prohibited them from sharing Jesus with the rest of us. Also, had the Jews adopted Christianity on a wholesale basis during the early centuries after Christ's crucifixion, they would have lost their identity. Their absorption by the surrounding gentile communities within which they were embedded would have been a fait accompli.

Jews preserved sacred truths.

Absent such absorption, the Temple's destruction and Jewish dispersion led to the proliferation of Jewish synagogues. Within those were found rabbinical teachers dedicated to the study and preservation of the Torah and Talmud from which comes our present Old Testament knowledge. It was Jewish dedication to the Law of Moses that held them together then, just as it does now. That dedication enabled them to preserve for all of us, in something approaching a pure form, what Christians call the Old Testament with its teachings and history. Without this counterbalancing preservation during Christianity's infancy, we might have lost those teachings and lore and might have seen the zeal of Christ's early followers skew their messages even more than they did.

Imperfect Words for a Perfect God

As Bart D. Ehrman persuades us in his book, *Misquoting Jesus*, we do not have the unalloyed words of Jesus or the Prophets today. There were no printers or printing presses around at the times the books of the Bible were written. Instead, there were only limited numbers of handwritten scrolls and letters that were copied with painstaking effort by scribes, one at a time. Most of the world's population in those times was illiterate and those hand-copied texts were read to them aloud in churches, synagogues, and mosques.

In the copying process that preserved and passed on these texts, it was all too easy for the copyist to either make a mistake or, in an attempt to fit those texts to the beliefs held by that copyist and his contemporaries, modify the words being transmitted. That was an all-too-prevalent practice. At the very end of Revelations, the last book of the New Testament, its author acknowledges the danger of unfounded reinterpretation and warns those who are so inclined:

> I myself give witness to all who hear the prophetic words of this book. If anyone adds to these words, God will visit him with all the plagues described herein! If anyone takes from the words of this prophetic book, God will take away his share in the tree of life and the holy city described here! [22;18-19]

Nonetheless, on page fifty two of *Misquoting Jesus*, Mr. Ehrman tells us that Origen, a third century church leader, was later forced to complain with bitterness,

> The differences among the manuscripts have become great, either through the negligence of some copyists or through the perverse audacity of others; they either neglect to check over what they have transcribed, or, in the process of checking, they make additions or deletions as they please.

Origen's claim can also be applied to the Koran and its use of Jewish thought and teachings. In fact, when you read the Koran you will note Jewish Biblical stories that have a new twist or changes to facts common to the earlier Christian Bible and Jewish Torah. For example, in the Koran it is Ishmael, Abraham's son by Haggar, whom God favored over Isaac. For Islam, it is Ishmael who is offered up for sacrifice on the rock by his father Abraham, not Isaac. Thus, according to Islamic doctrine, it is Ishmael's descendants, the Muslim nation, who correctly worship God, not the Judeo-Christians.

Jews' refusal to embrace Islam can be attributed to their conviction that neither the prophet Mohammed nor Islam itself represented their conception of the Messiah. Jewish independence and separateness was at least a partial check on any Christian or Islamic tendency to selectively translate or otherwise alter the Old Testament or the New to fit Christians' or Muslims' preconceived notions of what God's Word should be.

Jewish preservation of Old Testament teachings in effect provided a standard for accuracy against which comparisons could be and are made. Certainly, this is at least one of the reasons for what I would contend is God's desire for Judaism to remain forever distinct as a religion and people. It would seem that it is part of God's plan for Judaism to remain separate and apart from Christianity and Islam to function as a form of leaven down through the ages. In that capacity, Jews represent the importance of observance and of respect for laws that transcend nations. Their traditions enrich our thoughts and our cultures along the way; they've marked our past, they serve as signposts for us now, and they provide warnings to us about the future because there is much everyone still has to learn from their history. In that sense, they are, indeed, the Chosen People.

"Nonetheless, they crucified our Lord," some of us might still insist. "What should we do about it?" they demand in an attempt to cloak their own imperfection and incite others to purge what they want everyone to see as "evil." I believe we should ask, instead, what would have happened had Jesus not been crucified. Had he not experienced a horrible death, had he not been buried, and had he not risen from the dead, where would Christianity be today? Had the Jews and their leaders wholeheartedly accepted Jesus as their messiah during his lifetime, without his death and resurrection, where would we be?

Let us release the Jews from a prison so many have confined them to.

Jesus proved on the cross that he could, in fact, die. Without that, I doubt the rest of the world would have taken his Divinity seriously.

I'm convinced God engineered Christ's crucifixion and the subsequent Jewish rejection of Jesus so that we might know Christ and his teachings. If there is any blame to lay on Roman or Israelite, we should let God do the blaming and we should let Him decide what, if any, punishment should be rendered.

Let us release Jews and Judaism from a prison so many in the world have so self-righteously consigned them to. Let us acknowledge that all of us have blood on our hands, passed on from our forebears. It can't be washed off with someone else's blood, Jewish or otherwise. Let us free those persecuted people and free ourselves from the chains of bigotry, in whatever form it exists, so that we can, at last, stop killing Christ.

Judaism Permeates Our Lives

Despite our prejudices, Jewish beliefs, thought, and culture have survived and their influence has been so pervasive that we take it for granted. For example, the Jewish seven-day week, including a day of rest, has become the worldwide norm. Likewise, in nation after nation, many legal principles are, at heart, based on the Pentateuch—the first five books of the Old Testament: Genesis, Exodus, Leviticus, Numbers and Deuteronomy. Any lawyer reading them would comment, "That's my first year Property course from law school" or, "That's Torts 101."

Judaism's teachings have also affected our thinking in more subtle ways that we might not immediately recognize. You may or may not have noticed that I follow the Judeo-Christian practice of calling God "He" or "Him" and refer to "His" this or that. That practice is a product of Judaic theology.

Some years ago, a friend in South Africa sent me a letter in which she referred to God as "it," neither male nor female. Technically, I believe she is right. Obviously, God has no personal use for gender because He is the Supreme and eternal Being without other co-equal Gods. "He" has no need for male or female identity and their gender connotations.

Jesus' understanding of this fact is demonstrated in Mark 12:18-25. There we find the story of a group of Sadducees who tried to trap Jesus into contravention of the Law of Moses. At the same time, they demonstrated their belief in the impossibility of human resurrection. They posited to Jesus the conundrum of seven brothers who married the same woman in turn after the death of the preceding elder brother. Such Levirate or sequential marriage was required by their understanding of the Law of Moses to ensure the raising up of offspring in the deceased brother's name and the perpetuation of his line. The Sadducees told Jesus to assume that all involved had died, including the woman, without any of the unions producing a child, and they demanded that Jesus declare whose wife the woman would be after the resurrection. The Sadducees triumphantly concluded their supposition by reminding Jesus that she had, in turn, been married to all seven brothers. Making one of his few pronouncements on life in heaven, Jesus answered,

> You are badly misled, because you fail to understand the Scriptures or the power of God. When people rise from the dead, they neither marry nor are given in marriage but live like angels in heaven.

To me this means that there would not be a need in Heaven for offspring to carry on a mortal race. Therefore, gender and all of gender's drives and limitations would no longer matter there. But despite this understanding, I'm still not comfortable referring to God as "it."

Like most people who refer to God, I accept the Jewish practice of thinking of the Supreme Being as "Him." There is more of an explanation for this, however, than we just have to refer to God in some way. As a Christian, I believe God chose to come to Earth as the male named Jesus and return to Heaven in that same guise. His logic in doing this is irrefutable—He was presenting himself to a Judaic society that believed in and was dominated by male authority figures. Abraham, Isaac, and Jacob were the first of these and they passed the mantle on to Moses, Joshua, David, Solomon, and others over thousands of years. It was a society that longed for fulfillment of the scriptural prophecies that told of a future male "king" in the Davidic line who would be their Messiah.

Gender distinctions will disappear when they no longer matter.

In all four gospels, Jesus addresses God or refers to Him as "Father." Clearly, the culture of that time was totally male-oriented; a genderless Messiah was unthinkable. If God had appeared on Earth in the only other human choice, a female, His ministry would have never started. Though Jewish culture permitted female judges as temporary leaders and some females were considered to be prophetesses, a female of Jesus' time claiming to be the Messiah would have been seen as mad or as a creature of Satan.

Thus, when the risen Jesus ascended to Heaven to be reunited with God, we think of him as having taken his maleness with him. This early Judeo-Christian concept of a male God has left a lasting imprint on all of us. As we discussed earlier, we humans can only use the imperfect faculties, knowledge, and experiences that are available to us to describe and explain God. Referring to God as "it" not only contravenes these historical teachings, it implies He is inanimate and unintelligent. God is neither; He lives within each of us and His design is genius itself. Male and female is just His way to propagate our species so that humanity can continue His plan and may one day be one with Him. Gender is just another difference that will disappear when it no longer matters at all.

We should reflect on the meaning of the Biblical passage where the word "man" is just that—a word with no overriding connotations:

> God created man in his image;
> in the divine image he created him;
> male and female he created them. [Genesis 1:27]

Another passage further emphasizes the unified totality of male and female:

When God created man, he made him in the likeness
of God; he created them male and female.
When they were created he blessed them and named
them 'man'. [Genesis 5:1-2]

It is God who made us. Though we must refer to Him in some way, I'd contend that we should not impose on God human preconceptions of what His profile should be in any manner, including gender. When we do that it is we who are trying to remake God in our image instead of accepting the fact that it is the other way around. And no matter how hard we try to force God to conform to our limited thinking, we will fail.

Instead, I hope we can focus on the personal tasks God has assigned to each of us no matter which gender we identify with. Let us embrace and celebrate our gender differences as we try to meld them into a more perfect whole of humanity. If we recognize how the genders support, enhance each other as opposites, and fit together and act as counterbalances, I trust we will come closer to realizing God's spirit. That matters a lot more than how we describe Him.

On more than one occasion, God inspired his servant Paul to use the metaphor of the body and its parts to describe the whole that was and is the Christian Church. Paul emphasized that no one part was independent of, or truly better than, the others. And that includes genitalia. All were equally necessary to the functioning of the whole. Likewise, "man" is both male and female, a whole that God embodies and it is that whole we should focus on.

When we are fixated on gender, we miss the point that God created us together as "man." Mankind cannot go far without both genders working together in a partnership based on equal footing. We should set aside the baggage and implications of gender distinction we have laden ourselves with; we should ignore labels and seize another opportunity to eradicate differences and man-made assumptions that divide us. The challenge is to master personal flaws and recognize how much more God-like both man and woman are when they work together with equality as an unified whole.

FOUR

Condemn or Acquit—
Harvesting the Good

A s God shepherds humanity from ancient imperfection toward a more perfect future, He shepherds our faiths along the same path. Just as the Bible was written by imperfect beings, faiths were founded through the efforts of the fallible. For the most part, those foundations occurred thousands of years in the past. Christianity was formed almost two thousand years ago and Jesus' followers based major portions of their beliefs on Jewish scripture that was centuries older. Those who wrote the books of what became the Christian Bible, the Old and New Testaments, thought and understood in the contexts of their own limited knowledge of how the world and the Universe were constructed and how they functioned. Our ancestors were likewise constrained by their limited knowledge of other peoples and cultures.

While we assume that what they wrote was Divinely inspired, that inspiration would have, of necessity, been constrained by the limited amounts of accumulated human knowledge available at the time. It would have been useless for God to impart concepts based on quantum mechanics and sub-atomic particles, for example, to the authors of Genesis. They had no foundation for that as I am sure there is none now for the things that will be common knowledge in our distant future. Similarly, it would have been impossible for ancient people to comprehend the idea of tens of billions of years of time because they thought of existence and creation in terms of less than a hundred generations of human history that spanned only a couple of thousand years. But these were the people God had available at that time. They wrote as best they could not only about God's love, but also about other, often terribly imperfect, men and women.

When one thinks about it, the Bible is in significant part the story of how God utilizes flawed human beings to teach us and to implement His plan and purpose. Thus, He not only used imperfect authors to write scripture, but, of equal importance, He employed the incredibly flawed people we meet in chapter after chapter of the Bible's books to effectuate His purposes. God wove each of them and their imperfections into His design for advancing humankind down through the ages. The Bible's authors may have been imperfect, and its characters far from pure, but their attempts at recording God's message of love and the characters' striving to rise above their failings are instructive for all time.

God utilizes flawed humans to teach us.

To see this, all we have to do is open the Bible to The Book of Genesis and begin reading. To use but a few of the myriad examples we encounter there, we can start with the first two prototypical people we find depicted in the Bible, Adam and Eve. They and their downfall are the quintessential symbols for all of humanity's flaws. From there, it's easy to move on to Abraham who twice denied his marriage to his wife Sarah and turned her over to other men out of fear for his own hide. Next, we come to Jacob and the story of the theft of his brother Esau's birthright and blessing. These patterns of flawed human conduct are repeated page after page on down through the patriarchs, judges, and kings to David who, out of lust, committed murder. From there, we can go on to Solomon who let foreign gods into Israel to please some of his pagan wives. In chapter after chapter, the Bible recounts in detail the flaws and imperfections of those God uses to move His purposes and plan along.

The New Testament is no exception to this. For example, during his life Jesus' own brothers, after doubting and rejecting him, became founding figures in Christianity. Paul himself persecuted the Christian Church until he was struck by God on that fateful road to Damascus.

The authors of Scripture spoke for God as best they could.

We learn that God has always worked with what He had at hand: imperfect men and women with a limited and far from perfect knowledge base. As the authors of scripture and the characters in His drama, those women and men had rather minimal frames of reference to assist them in conceptualizing what God imparted to them. To them, the Sun revolved around a flat, not round, Earth, and the stars were not other suns and galaxies but little points of light hung on some sort of huge dome-like ceiling, and Heaven was above that. To them, time was divided into day and night, lunar months, and seasons of the year—not eons. Out of these perceptions came the scriptures we have today. The authors of those scriptures tried, as best they could, to speak for God, to prophesy in the words of the Bible. But they could only prophesy in terms their contemporaries, reading what was written, could understand.

To paraphrase what Paul so eloquently declared on behalf of all those who prophesy in the name of God:

> (Their) knowledge (was) imperfect and (their) prophesying (was) imperfect. When the perfect comes, the imperfect will pass away. [I Corinthians 13:9-10]

When Paul was a child he used to "talk like a child, think like a child, reason like a child." When he became a man he put childish ways aside. He "saw indistinctly as in a mirror [of polished brass] and his and their knowledge was imperfect then."[I Corinthians 13:11-12]

I would suggest that we must read what Paul and all those others who wrote or prophesied on behalf of God said as if they were both a bit childish and a bit imperfect in terms of the concepts and the limited frames of reference that they had to communicate their ideas and beliefs to the world. We have to separate the basic truths they imparted about faith, hope, and love from the unsophisticated notions the scriptures deliver those truths with.

The imperfect knowledge of our ancestors has now been improved by our more-enlightened science-based understanding. But, lest we boast, we should keep in mind that significant parts of our knowledge base will in its turn be modified and improved as future generations produce even more accurate and acute learning. As we are currently constrained by the limits of scientific and spiritual knowledge in understanding God, His laws and His purposes, those who went before us were even more confined in their thinking. The ancients did the very best that they could with their imperfection. And we must do the same with ours.

Separating Wheat from Chaff

As humankind has advanced from the places and times of original Scripture, each generation has had to struggle with the meaning and import of the words found in the God-inspired writings they inherited. As part of that struggle, critics such as Richard Dawkins in *The God Delusion,* Sam Harris in *The End of Faith,* and Christopher Hitchens in *God Is Not Great* have been correct in pointing out that this tortured effort has, from time to time right down to the present, led groups of believers and even entire nations into protracted episodes of perversion of their faiths. The Spanish Inquisition, Salem witch hunts, South African Apartheid, and the Taliban come to mind in this regard. But a narrow concentration on the tales of intrigue, killing, destruction, war, and Divine retribution that are part of religious history and the human condition ignores the accounts of miraculous happenings that accompany those tales. When this is done, I believe a basic characteristic of human nature, whether ancient or modern, is missed.

Dawkins, Harris, and Hitchens conclude from faith's bloody history that religious belief itself is evil and the root of many, if not all, of the modern world's ills. By doing so, they choose to ignore the messages of love, compassion, service to neighbors, and the greater call to righteous conduct that are woven throughout faith's scriptures. They throw out the baby with the bath water, as our modern media does every day in its focus on vice and tragedy for higher ratings. Any survey of the fare served up on our television screens, in our movie theaters, in novels, and on the pages of our newspapers more than amply demonstrates that the worst aspects of human nature rivet attention and interest. It is gory depictions of chain saw massacres, mayhem, war, revenge, witches and warlocks, and conflict in all its human guises that fascinates the vast majority of the world's populace. People just can't seem to get enough of it.

We don't pay sufficient attention to the good stuff.

We don't pay sufficient attention to the good stuff. The fact that a small locale such as Junction City, Kansas, is an ordinary, peaceful little Midwest town that goes along, year after year, in its law-abiding ways is of no interest to us. But when a Timothy McVey rented the truck there that he later used to blow up the Oklahoma City Federal Building, snuffing out hundreds of innocent lives, Junction City became a center of our focus under a swarm of reporters. It was trumpeted in every media outlet all across the world because of its association with something violent that held our attention for a long time.

Similarly, compilations of rules, regulations, and admonitions contained in the oldest law books are routinely ignored or forgotten by the very people they were supposed to help. In fact, philosophical dissertations on probity and virtue will downright put most of us to sleep; it has been ever so. I'm sure God accepts this part of our imperfect natures. Thus, I would argue that He inspired the tales of miracles and mayhem found in scripture for the very purpose advertisers use them today—to grab our attention so that once captured, the less-titillating messages of love and right conduct can be imparted to those of us who have short attention spans.

Messages of love are often ignored.

Not unlike myths of yore, the Bible, along with many other religious texts, presents higher truths via stories of imperfect human conduct and eye-popping disaster. They are a means to get us flawed humans to focus on and internalize truths. Because they are embedded in these stories, we can relate to them as they grab our attention. Many overlook this possibility. Instead, they jump to the conclusion that the horrific side of scriptural tales demonstrates with certainty that there can be no God. They argue that no God worth His salt would allow such bloody events to occur. He would, instead, protect each of us and the rest of humanity from such calamities. In doing so, however, they fall into the trap we have already discussed, that of believing God would exist only to serve us. They make flawed humans the masters and a perfect God the servant who meekly stands by to do our bidding as if He were some sort of genie in a lamp. I have suggested that the truth is just the opposite—it is we who are here to serve God and each other despite all of our imperfections.

God has existed forever—long before the first word of scripture was ever penned; He always was, and shall always be. Atheists and others confuse religion with God. Religions are not God; human words and ideas cannot define or adequately represent an infinite God who existed long before any human or religion showed up. Instead, religions represent humanity's varied struggles over the millennia to understand and relate to God and His teachings. In this struggle, we imperfect humans have all too often misused religion just as we have misused so much else in our lives. But that does not make our struggles to understand God or the concept of good vs. evil invalid. Nor does it prove that God is just a figment of our imagination.

God's existence or non-existence is not dependent on the accuracy of sacred writings.

God's existence or non-existence is not dependent on the accuracy of the Christian Bible, the Islamic Koran, the teachings of Buddha, or the Hindu Sruti. It is not dependent on any single piece of human writing or the sum total of all that has been recorded. The Bible and humanity's other religious texts are only flawed frameworks intended to act as springboards to launch our equally-imperfect efforts at grasping the nature of God and His purpose for every human being. They are our poor, but well-intended, efforts to teach each other about God and His purpose and plan for our existence.

I would argue that people should use scripture in all its forms as vehicles for thinking about God as we try to understand our relationship with Him and the relationships we should have with each other. Over the millennia, these efforts have engendered both success and failure. We flawed humans have followed a tortured and far from straight-line advancement, starting as hardly more than beasts, crouched and snarling over our kill or stumbled-upon carrion, fearful that some other creature would steal them from us, to the point of being willing to share with and protect those other creatures. Scripture has played no small part in encouraging and illuminating this advance.

The Misuse of Faith

From the dawn of time, humans have been attracted to mystery by a deeply-ingrained sense that there was something or someone far greater who guided our efforts. We have been drawn to God by whatever names we have called Him down through the ages. Admittedly, as flawed as we are, we often misused this attraction to the mystery that is God to justify our exclusion, persecution, and even destruction of other humans who hold differing beliefs. But to leap from this misuse to the conclusion that God does not exist and faith is evil is flawed logic. In the words of Francis Collins, the scientist who led the Human Genome Project, "We shouldn't judge the pure truths of faith by the way they are applied any more than we should judge the pure truths of love by an abusive marriage."

I believe that God wishes us nothing but good. To me, using faith to justify harming other human beings is to twist and deform that which God teaches all of humanity—to have faith and hope in Him, and to love everyone. It is a misunderstanding of how God wants us to treat each other and a perversion of His plan for all of mankind. If we use faith to blindly justify the subjugation or killing of others who believe in something different from that which we have been taught to believe, we misinterpret the meaning God attaches to faith. Faith is belief in something we can't empirically prove but trust is true. Extremism based on faith is a destructive abomination of that faith; the Inquisition and suicide bombers are just two manifestations of this phenomenon. Faith cannot be the justification for wrong. To use faith in God to spread evil is to desecrate both faith and God.

Thus, faith walks a fine line. We humans are drawn to faith and need it. But faith, to be true to itself, cannot ignore the hard facts of reality or the difficult choices that confront humanity. Using faith to ignore or deny truth and to justify avoiding the confrontation of destructive threats to humanity's future is also a perversion of belief. When this happens, faith becomes delusion.

Faith must not ignore the hard facts.

Faith requires ethical choices. We must not compel "true" belief or "true" faith by either force or violence. At best, they only produce outward conformity that conceals a hidden hatred of others. Using faith to justify evil acts is to corrupt that faith. Belief has to be arrived at voluntarily by each person; otherwise, it is only a sham and a perversion of what it is supposed to stand for. This is especially true when brutality in the name of faith is the instrument used to coerce acquiescence. Not unlike child abuse that often produces the next generation of child abusers, those who are forced to believe through brutality, threats, and fear tend to pass on their faith in the same manner. Faith that is generated as a product of violence is flawed and deformed, the opposite of what God has taught us, and such malice leads to its own destruction.

Abuses of faith are human failings, not the failings of God. Nonetheless, nonbelievers consider this imperfect human conduct and argue that it justifies rejection of all faith and proves that a perfect God does not exist. They posit that faith has no purpose and should be replaced with non-theistic rational human conduct based on pure reason as defined by scientists and philosophers. This, they argue, would correct all of humankind's flawed faith-based conduct. They make the assumption that the bloody acts they rightly abhor would have never occurred or won't be repeated in the future in the absence of faith. They don't acknowledge humanity's extensive history of barbaric behavior that was unrelated to faith of any kind. I would suggest that they need to do so. The French Revolution that arose out of the Age of Enlightenment, led by philosophers who tried to change human conduct in the name of "reason," is a prime example. It didn't work.

Abuses of faith are human failings, not the failings of God.

Referring to those secular intellectual leaders who included such great minds as Rousseau and Voltaire, the famous French historian and social observer Alex de Tocqueville wrote:

> They all think that it would be good to substitute basic and simple principals, derived from reason and natural law, for the complicated and traditional customs which ruled the societies of their times.

One of the principal customs de Tocqueville was referring to was organized religion with all its warts. He went on to write that,

> Without doubt, the universal discredit into which all religious beliefs fell at the end of the last [eighteenth] century exercised the greatest influence on the whole of

our Revolution; it marked its character. Nothing did more
to give its features the terrible expression we have seen.

That "terrible expression" was one of despotism, a reign of terror, and extensive use of the guillotine. One of de Tocqueville's biographers, Joseph Epstein, from whom I borrowed the preceding quotes, writes on page one-hundred-seventy-six of *Alex de Tocqueville: Democracy's Guide*,

...without God, men had only themselves to fall back
on, and fall back on themselves they did; under the new
dispensation, the state, not God, would make man.

The revolutionary French government did away with religion and substituted in its place the reign of Reason. The result, as chronicled by two eminent historians, Will and Ariel Durant, in Volume X of their monumental *The Story of Civilization*, on page eight-hundred-ninety-nine, was that:

We cannot doubt that the philosophers profoundly
affected the ideology and the political drama of the
Revolution. They had not intended to produce violence,
massacre and the guillotine; they would have shrunk in
horror from those bloody scenes. They could properly
say that they had been cruelly misunderstood; but they
were responsible insofar as they had underestimated
the influences of religion and tradition in restraining
the animal instincts of men.

Other movements and secular ideologies have similarly rejected religious restraints as part of their ethos with equally devastating results. German National Socialism as practiced by Adolph Hitler, the Marxism-Leninism of the Soviet Union and Communist China, Cambodia's killing fields under Pol Pot's Khmer Rouge, Cuba under Castro, Kim Jong-il's North Korea, and the tribal warfare-produced massacres of Tutsis by the Hutus of Rwanda—so chillingly described by Jared Diamond in *Collapse*—are more than enough examples to consider on this point.

Richard Dawkins and others would counter these arguments by classifying Communism and perhaps German National Socialism as the equivalents of faiths. This argument, however, raises an interesting corollary. It seems to me that any reading of Dawkins' *God Delusion* and Hitchens' *God Is Not Great* leads to the conclusion that a belief in atheism is the equivalent for them of religious faith, one they would convert the rest of the world to. So it would seem that we are all drawn to faith in one form or other. But as a faith, atheism is just as flawed as all of our other faiths when applied by imperfect human beings.

Rising Above Conflict

History has revealed our ability to pervert any and all belief systems, no matter what their base, be it religious faith, political philosophy, or reason. We humans have repeatedly demonstrated that we are capable of irrational violence in either the name of religious belief or in the name of political or social dogma. None of this proves or disproves the existence of God, however, despite all the arguments put forth by atheists. What it does do is produce counterbalancing forces whose pull against each other is part of what advances human development. We should consider the arguments raised by all sides, religious and atheist alike, in an attempt to discern valid points about the imperfections of our beliefs. We must not hide from those flaws in our own individual belief systems that such confrontations expose. We do not have to make excuses for the imperfect human authors who set down the scriptures on which we base our beliefs, whatever they may be. As the Durants noted above, those authors can justly claim in their own defense that they have from time to time been cruelly misunderstood.

To use a hackneyed phrase, truth does set us free. It opens our eyes and our hearts and our minds. Therefore, we should not fear truth nor avoid facts. Instead, we should use them to expand our beliefs and advance thereby as a race. We must adopt the best concepts regardless of their origin and lead our faiths away from their historic imperfections and conflicts. As I see it, to do that and not be repressive, a faith must have enough elasticity to allow for increased understanding and spiritual growth in the light of facts, ideas, and concepts as they immerge out of our collective human learning and experience. When a faith rigidly demands conformity to precepts and social norms that may have been needed or accepted yesterday or thousands of years ago, but hinder or deny mankind's true needs today, it freezes people in patterns of existence that are stultifying, making it impossible for believers to deal in a loving way with the world in which they live.

Faith must have elasticity.

Thomas Friedman, in his book *The World Is Flat*, cites the example of those among the Muslims who believe the Koran's dictates, set down more than thirteen hundred years in the past, are the last and inflexible commands of God that must be rigidly obeyed at all costs, including the taking of human life. History has demonstrated that the individuals who conform to this thinking cannot grow beyond the point of human development achieved centuries ago. When the rest of the world passes them by, leaving them humiliated in disrespected backwaters of mental and emotional existence, they react with rage and try to hold back their own societies and the rest of the world with increased determination—and violence. These are the people who become the suicide bombers and terrorists. They go on to attack those who have moved much further forward after thirteen-hundred years of intellectual growth.

Contrary to their thinking, God's desire and plan for humanity, in all of its divergent components, springs from love. He wants us to grow, develop, and mature; to shed, little by little, our imperfections. Different faiths are part of His grand design that helps us on our journey from imperfection towards perfection.

Out of love, I would gladly include atheism among those faiths because its adherents have forced me to think about faith in ways I had never considered before. I hope I can do the same for them. In the end, all of us, atheists and believers alike, are striving for the same thing: a better and more just future for all of humanity. Differences between and among people are a given; the challenge is to acknowledge common goals and work together, however imperfectly, toward that future.

Imperfect Striving Toward Perfection

Throughout history, only a couple of humans have ever been thought of as perfect. A large part of the world would put Buddha on that very short list and many others would identify Christ as the quintessential role model. Moslems, as I understand it, name Mohammed as the ultimate prophet, albeit infallible only in the words of the Koran he dictated at the direction of an angel of God. As for the rest of us, we are quite imperfect and often blind to our own flaws and shortcomings—more proof of how imperfect we are. But many claim perfection and demand it from others, yet are afraid when they think they are in its presence.

The best example of fearing perfection is Christ himself. As flawed as we are, I think humanity couldn't tolerate being challenged by his perfection, so we crucified Him. Moreover, I feel the world continues to crucify him today as many imitate the Pharisees of his time. It is still all too easy to tell those around us to do as we say and ignore what we and our institutions do. So I'd ask us to consider how often we demand perfection from others while discounting our own shortcomings, how we fail to lead by example, by action, instead of by hollow words.

I'm convinced we need to accept the inherent human flaws and the neuroses, insecurities and other imperfections in every person and in every society and faith we are a part of. Then we need to acknowledge how well we function despite these limitations.

God wants us to shed all imperfections, including flawed expressions of faith.

For example, in the past few years there have been a flurry of biographies on Benjamin Franklin, John Adams, John Marshall, and other "Founding Brothers" of America. These studies have exposed the foibles, vanities, and glaring imperfections of accomplished, but all-too-human, leaders. Reading them, one realizes that Adams could be accused of being judgmental and a prig; Franklin, a dirty old man; Jefferson, a hypocrite. Yet we celebrate the incredible achievements of these imperfect statesmen, all of whom benefit us to this day.

What God does—individual-by-individual, generation-by-generation, and institution-by-institution—is help us be a little bit better than those who came before us. He is working humanity through imperfection towards a perfection that is the highest form of existence. It seems to me that He wants us to experience and understand our own flaws and fallibility first. They're the "fire" that shapes and hardens our "mettle." I believe He wants us to face and acknowledge these shortcomings, first to ourselves and then to those around us. In my case, I have my own share of flaws and faults, not the least of which are a Pharisee's sort of self-satisfaction on occasion, and, contrary to what I've counseled against here and more often than I'd prefer, a nagging need for the recognition of others.

I believe that as long as we are imperfect, God wants us to give up demanding perfection from others and work on our own shortcomings. This is especially true in the way we tend to pass judgment on those who are just trying to help or please us, such as spouses, children, subordinates, teachers, clergy, and politicians. I would hope we can let God be the judge of their failure to be absolutely perfect, not us. Each of us has more than enough inside ourselves to worry about and to get busy fixing.

I am confident that in an imperfect world we can learn to deal with imperfection in a loving way. That does not mean ignoring it or condoning it. What it does mean is forgiving imperfection in others as we try to overcome it in ourselves, our societies, and in our faiths, too. With this in mind, I propose the best way to surmount our limitations is through positive reinforcement. I believe that I can do better and my fellow humans can do better, too. I have a plan for how I will improve, you can devise your own, and we can follow our own advice.

Does it really matter how one chooses to profess a universal truth?

What we can't do is to give in to exasperation with ourselves or with those who are leading us, or with those we lead or teach. How many times has each of us become annoyed or angry with somebody who didn't do something as well as we convince ourselves we could have done it? And how often do those feelings express themselves in our snide backbiting of a leader or someone we work or interact with? When we act with intolerance toward others, we ignore our own imperfections and forget that others are not us. Each person has an individual set of abilities and limitations. It is up to us as followers, leaders, teachers, or motivators to feel out what the maximum extent of those abilities and limitations is. Then we can help that individual perform as best as possible, which can be far higher than he or she dreams is achievable or despairs about reaching. Remember: the function of any group or organization is to maximize its collective strengths while compensating for individual weaknesses.

When we lead best, we get each person under our care to perform up to the limits of imperfect capabilities. Alternatively, when we are in the role of followers, we must encourage those who are leaders to recognize their own limitations and help them compensate for those deficiencies, not just ridicule and complain about them.

Recognizing the universality of human imperfection, we have to ask ourselves, as we discussed before, what makes us so sure that ours is the perfect "ism" or opinion or brand of politics? What makes us think that our faith is the one and only true one, unquestionably leading us toward the future God has outlined for all of humanity? If there are universal truths as is commonly accepted, does it really matter how one chooses to profess and observe them?

Common Origins and Destination

I'm reminded of an incident a Jewish client and friend of mine recounted to me in the mid 1970s. The ancestors on one side of his family were Sephardic Jews from North Africa and he had always been fascinated with the area, so he decided to tour Morocco where they originated. On that trip, he and his wife were being chauffeured through the Atlas Mountains on their way to the famous, ancient city of Marrakech in the high desert. A part of his family had once lived there and had left more than two hundred years before.

My friend and his wife stopped in a small village to buy water and a snack when one of the villagers noticed the Star of David the wife was wearing on her charm bracelet. My friend heard hostile muttering from the small crowd that seemed to form from nowhere and the only words he could understand from the babble that grew louder and angrier by the second was the phrase for "Jew." The leader of what my friend feared was becoming a mob demanded that the driver tell the crowd whether the two foreigners were, in fact, Jews. So my friend, speaking through the driver, told them yes, he was a Jew and was on a journey to pay homage in the city that had given shelter and water to his ancestors many years before. He said that he knew those in the crowd around him were Muslims and that he had started his journey from a city that was Christian. He told them that he would like to think that his and their ancestors had all started on their own journeys, no matter where they lived, from the same place—the heart, as he and his wife had—and were all searching for the same thing: God and a better world.

We are all "peoples of the book."

My client went on to say that during those quests, some had elected to take the coastal route where they could see, as they searched for a new home, the magnificence of God reflected in the sea and upon the towering cliffs that overlooked the ocean. Others had chosen to follow the roads through the high mountains where they were spurred on by the beauty of God that was apparent on the mountain peaks and in the crystal clear high mountain air. A third group had opted for the desert trails where they could discern God in the stark simplicity of that barren environment. My friend expressed the hope that those listening to him could accept the fact that no matter what they called themselves or believed they were all seeking the same destination and home—God and His wisdom—but that he and they, like their ancestors before them, had just elected to follow different paths to the same goal and dream.

As my friend's driver translated the story, the small crowd had grown quieter. When he finished, they all heaved a collective sigh. The man who had been asking the questions begrudged the hasty bow he made toward my friend, touching hand to his forehead, lips, and heart in rapid succession before he thanked my friend for being a great teacher and reminding him that they were all "peoples of the book." With that, my friend, his wife, and the driver were allowed to go on their way with at least a bit more toleration, if not outright acceptance.

Every belief must withstand scrutiny.

For any belief, religious or secular, to be true, it must withstand scrutiny. It must be put to the test of what others have to say about it. If it's false, it might last for multiple generations, but it won't be around long if we consider the true span of time. Even though we're in our relative infancy as a race, there have already been quite of few "isms," such as feudalism, Nazism, and Communism that have fallen to the wayside. It is hoped that religious fanaticism will join those soon.

God guides our development as we guide a child's development. He provides rules and direction as He lets us make choices, decisions, and mistakes as part of our individual and collective growth. If we choose to hide in fear or intimidation from the challenges of other faiths, from the absence of faith, or from the multitude of political philosophies God has seen fit to allow on this Earth, I'm convinced we will never truly overcome our personal limitations and imperfections and those of whatever faith we have. We'll lose the opportunity to gain added strength from the good of others that is needed for the grueling struggle to attain collective salvation.

We should keep in mind always that no matter where one might be on salvation's evolutionary scale, each of us is flawed in our own way. But if we embrace an understanding of our imperfections (I'm reminded of Don Corleone's advice to keep your friends close but your enemies closer), use them as the impetus for tolerance of others and acceptance of what we can all achieve, we will keep the hope alive that we will harvest one day the good that God has engendered in everyone.

FIVE

Form or Substance— Reaching Common Ground

If we do not believe that there is a God who dispenses guidance, love, and forgiveness, our vision of life is narrowed to the here and now. Existence itself becomes coarsened and far bleaker, which often leads to emptiness and destruction. If we have faith, there is hope for the future, and we can rise above that coarseness and overcome the bleakness that abounds in this world.

But faith alone is not enough. We must combine faith with genuine spirituality. Many people don't understand the difference and often confuse the two. Faith is a belief in God, Yahweh, Allah, the Hindu Deities, or another Supreme Being, or in a concept such as Nirvana. Some of us believe in only one of these as the true faith, while others embrace multiple combinations. Spirituality, on the other hand, is how we relate to the God we have faith in. It is how we interact and communicate with God, our personal connection with the Divine.

When there is only rigid adherence to dogma, faith can be a dark and dreary thing that produces nothing but negative consequences— conflict, violence, and subjugation of the free will that is paramount for the preservation of hope and attainment of salvation. In my experience, when there is true spiritual communion, selflessness abounds and faith becomes the beautiful living and growing connection God wants it to be. And I don't think that connection is limited to any specific faith, no matter how much some might believe otherwise.

For example, I'm Christian, but I cannot deny that the Dalai Lama is truly spiritual. There is a linkage radiating between him and the Divine even if it is not based on my beliefs. I like to think that the Dalai Lama is communing with the God I believe in; he just views Him through different concepts, calls Him by a different name, and worships Him as a Buddhist with all of the differences that entails. But his spiritual interaction is real and undeniable as are his messages of hope and oneness. Rather than battle over which faith is right and which is wrong, people should first find within themselves the peace and tranquility that the Dalai Lama has, and then world peace will begin to take care of itself.

Faith can be a living and growing connection.

Based on my personal observations, I'd say individual spirituality is unique, even within the same faith where it differs in at least subtle ways from one person to the next, depending on personality, needs, and ability to connect with God. While the paths of other believers may be wrong for some, they are not necessarily wrong for those who follow them. By accepting them as just who they are—other human beings on their own quest for connection with the God we profess to love—we can learn from the good things they may have to offer from their search and experiences, without forcing them to agree or disagree with our truths. I am confident that among the spiritual wisdom and alternative practices others embody are real insights into how we can better connect with God. Using this collective wisdom enhances our own spirituality.

A Conversation with God

How do we establish and fully develop individual spirituality? I'm sure the ways are as varied as humanity itself. The way to start is to really talk with God in prayer, as I finally got around to doing in 1989 during that ten-day retreat at St. Joseph's Abbey I mentioned in the Introduction. It was ironic how the silent walls of that holy place, walls that enclosed me in a very small physical space, exposed the immeasurable dimension of spirituality and hope that warmed my very being. I had been a believer for most of my first five decades on Earth, but my spirituality began to truly bloom when I came to the realization that from then on I was to try to understand God and what He wanted from me.

A real conversation with the Almighty involves breaking down the walls around our hearts and shedding all pride and pretense that we are in ultimate control of our lives. When we let Him in, we embody the kind of spirituality that transcends time, place, and faith itself and renews hope within our souls. Only then do we find out what His purpose is for each of us, as I began to find out those twenty years or so ago.

A dialogue with God should be centered on an honest search for understanding. To open the lines of spiritual communication with Him, I recommend reading the Bible or other inspirational writings one page at a time, thinking about the underlying meaning of the words, and welcoming God into your heart. Take that first step, and the rest of them will come a lot easier.

A conversation with God should include what you know and feel about yourself and the world and what doesn't make sense to you. Ask Him how you can serve Him and your fellow man. Then go about your life and listen for His voiceless reply. I've been surprised at how often it is there or how it comes to me later in the most unexpected ways—at an event, in an article I am drawn to, or via a comment by friends or strangers that may not have been as significant to them as it was to me. Just like that, I'd recognize that my dialogue with God, the heart-to-heart talk that He wants me to focus on, is ongoing. You'll find the same thing in your life when spirituality takes over.

Ask God how you can serve Him.

In your exchange with God, think about how you conform to His teachings, and ask Him to help you understand why you have fallen short. Be open to His responses that might come in unexpected ways from unexpected sources because I'm convinced they are there if you are willing to recognize them. The problem is, all too often we're searching for them in all the wrong places or don't hear them because they aren't what we want them to be.

Spirituality is far more than memorization and recital of specific doctrines of faith. It is about feeling God's presence in our hearts and souls and about consideration for every one of His children. I've come to appreciate that God communicates with us through pure feelings: love, caring, approval, disapproval, shame, joy, patience worn thin, even anger. When we listen to these feelings, letting ourselves become attuned to them, we can recognize the nuances of their meaning in our daily lives.

As the Psalmist in the Old Testament and the author of Hebrews in the New Testament remind us: "Today, if you should hear His voice, harden not your hearts." [Psalms 95:7-8, Hebrews 4:7] Listen for God's voice with your mind and your heart. I believe you must hear Him with both to begin understanding His message to you. I'm sure that hearing Him with only one or the other isn't enough. If people listen with only their minds and address God in purely intellectual terms, I suspect they become "a noisy gong, a clanging cymbal," as Paul says in I Corinthians 13:1. He goes on to say in the next verse that if you "have the gift of prophecy and, with full knowledge, comprehend all mysteries, if (you) have faith great enough to move mountains," but you lack love and the other feelings of an emotional, heart-to-heart contact with both God and your fellow human beings, you are "nothing."

Listen for God's voice with your mind and your heart.

In the same vein, if we ignore our intellect and hear God with only our heart, we will drift on a sea of emotions or get lost in a fog of unreality. God's message to us is concrete and real; it must be identified and applied with reason and must be carried with love, caring, and respect—with feeling.

Those who say "Bah, humbug" to both faith and spirituality should ask themselves why they do so. Why do they profess a different faith— the nonexistence of God? I suspect it is because they are unable to believe in something they cannot see, hear, feel, or touch—something they can't produce a scientific explanation for. They don't, or can't, believe in God because they don't believe there is any physical proof of his existence.

Invisible Proof

In response, I propose folks consider the current state of the world's scientific understanding, an understanding that is far greater than that available to the human authors of our various religious texts in ages gone by. We now agree that there are many things that we cannot see, feel in a discreet way, or touch that we nonetheless know and accept as being real. Why? Because we can see and understand their effects. Obvious examples are gravity, subatomic particles, and antimatter. No one has ever seen them, but in everyday life or through empirical research, those outside and within the scientific community have seen the results of their presence. By this I mean the impact they have on other things, their telltale tracks of cause and effect.

In a similar manner, I would suggest a spiritual exercise of looking back over the course of your life for the tracks of God's presence in it. As we have acknowledged, we cannot see God or touch Him as a physical entity at any given moment in time. But if we examine our individual lives and history, we can see proof of His active presence on both the micro level of our personal lives and the macro level of society's historical march through time.

Remember the example of God's formation of Christianity I outlined earlier? God went through great lengths to create just the right setting, peoples, and belief systems that both accepted and rejected Jesus as Messiah. God's invisible hand ensured that Jesus' teachings would be based on and yet forced out of Judaism into the surrounding pagan world in such a manner that we descendants of those pagans are now the heirs of one of the world's great religions.

On another level, all of us have experienced the frustration of pounding on closed and bolted doors as we pursued careers or personal relationships that, in hindsight, we have come to realize weren't right for us. How often in that process have we sagged, in frustration or despair, against some mental wall only to find that instead of a wall, it was an unseen and open door we'd been ignoring? You see, it is God who bolts some doors and opens others even though we can't see Him doing it. It's His invisible hand that guides us to and through them.

God's invisible hand guides us.

This has happened to me on any number of occasions. The one I alluded to in the introduction profoundly changed the course of my life. As a young Naval Officer, I had applied to be admitted to the Navy's nuclear propulsion engineering program run by Admiral Hyman Rickover. But I was turned down (correctly, I might add) based on my mediocre engineering course grades at the Naval Academy. Without being nuclear propulsion-qualified, I could never command one of the Navy's nuclear submarines. Instead of what I had wanted, I was sent to Polaris submarine navigators school to learn inertial navigation. As I was not willing to accept this limitation on my future career potential in the Navy, I decided to leave the service and go to law school.

In hindsight, that was probably the best thing that could have happened to me. I have loved my career in the law as well as all the other avenues that have opened up to me as a result, including, and of most importance to me, marriage to my beloved Patricia. Without my having been turned away from a naval career I would in all likelihood have never crossed paths with her. So I am convinced I truly belong where I am and devoutly believe it is where God has wanted me to be.

We can *see the effects of God's work.*

I can see the trail of God's presence in my affairs and in those of the world around me. The cause and effect of His work on our behalf is there for us to see like tracks in a winter morning's snow outside our door—proof that something unseen has passed our way in the night. And, of equal significance, we can also see the disastrous effect of His absence from our lives and the lives of others who surround us. Just as we do not consciously sense the presence of gravity, but would immediately know if it were no longer there, when we disconnect from our spiritual tether to God, we are left floating in a meaningless emptiness without anchor or worthwhile purpose to our existence.

I believe that it is through faith and spirituality that hope is renewed, and it is through those unquantifiable forces that we come to know that God exists and to discover His true purpose for us. Connection to God allows Him to work His beneficial and healing wonders on our behalf. By and large, we do not see or feel that contact in a tangible way when it occurs. However, if we take the time to look we, like scientists, can see its effect, the trail marks it has left in our lives. And that is proof enough for me of God's existence.

It is up to each of us to participate in our becoming whole by joining our spiritual and faith-based selves, nurturing both sides of the equation until they are one, and then joining with others who are doing likewise with whatever faith they profess. Many people participate in our instruction, but it starts with teaching ourselves first that the burden of faith is the obligation to put it to good use with spirituality, in fellowship with everyone who shares the message of hope.

Many Roads Lead to God

No one group should assume that it has the God-given correct answers to what constitutes faith and spirituality. Any survey of the rest of humanity would show that there are far more people out there with different, but just as deeply held beliefs, than there are those who share the ones we call our own. This is true no matter who "we" is. Even those religions that have a billion or more followers, such as Islam and Christianity, represent only a minority of all people who believe in God or don't. That is why it makes more sense to convert oneself and strive to be a better person every day than it does to force personal beliefs onto as many others as one can just to increase the number of those who conform to a given belief.

Don't get me wrong—there's nothing wrong with sharing our faiths with others. But it has to be done with those who have opened their hearts and are ready to hear the message. After all, Jesus never sought to force anyone to accept God's new way. He simply laid out the message for those who were ready to hear his words.

From my point of view, all faiths share basic tenets: worship of the divine, love is paramount, live with high morals and do good deeds, share with others, and oppose evil. Opposing evil, by the way, isn't only done on a large scale using whatever weapons we have at our disposal; it's done on the smallest of scales when we strike ill will from our hearts and indecent thoughts from our minds, and when we stay our hands from wicked deeds. Humanity has woven these God-taught, worthy precepts into a myriad of faiths. So how could only one of them be authentic?

All faiths share basic tenets.

Men and women have tried to answer that question for millennia as they continued trying to win others to their point of view. There have been prolonged armed conflicts and loss of life over who was right and who was wrong. This is ongoing today as many seek the one faith that will attain universal acceptance and approval from the rest of humankind. But no one has succeeded in this quest and it occurs to me that it might never happen. The simple explanation may be that God just doesn't want there to be only one answer.

God's attitude towards this sort of uniformity may be found in one of the stories He inspired, the "Tower of Babel," set forth in Genesis 11:1-9. In verse 1, its authors posited that there was a time when "the whole world spoke the same language, using the same words;" there was only one people. In their pride, they wanted to build a structure high enough to reach God, but their obsession missed the point of how they could do that. God was displeased; He confused their language so they could no longer understand one another. Their ambitious project came to a halt and these proud people were scattered over the Earth.

God wants us to reach Him via our hearts.

God did not want humanity to advance in lockstep down through history and experience social and spiritual evolution with everyone focused on saying, doing, and believing the same thing. Instead, He fostered diversity and wants all of us to reach Him in our own way—via the heart that He gave to all of us. That is the only way to eliminate all differences.

Force and Counterforce

So why hasn't one set of values, beliefs, and lifestyle come to dominate the entire world after all this time, if there is but one true God as I believe? Why this need for opposites and opposition that God seems to foster? I am persuaded the reason for that is human beings need opposites and healthy opposition to balance and challenge us so that we may grow. From the beginning of time down to the present day, human life is a series of counterbalanced opposites: men and women; black, white, and brown (and all the variations thereof); farmers and city dwellers; liberals and conservatives; capitalists and communists; Hindus, Jews, Moslems, Protestants, and Catholics; believers and nonbelievers. An argument can be made that the reason for this is that without such opposing forces, we humans tend to take our beliefs to unchecked extremes, as the architects and builders of the Tower of Babel did. Such extremes corrupt the very beliefs they arise from and those who believe in them. And I do not think that is part of God's plan at all.

Consider the more recent example of a powerful group that is absolutely sure it has the one and only true answer – the Taliban. These extremists hijacked the faith of Islam and are trying to return it, along with the nations of Afghanistan and Pakistan, to the twelfth century. Calling themselves students, they forbade the education of women and girls and reduced females to the status of property or cattle. Music and most other forms of entertainment, including such innocent pastimes as kite flying, were banned. As part of their certainty, the Taliban sought to eliminate all countervailing belief systems, even slightly less rigid expressions of Islam that they felt inhibited the growth of their extreme retrograde version of Mohammed's teachings.

God did not allow such fanatics to flourish unchecked. After the horror of September 11, 2001 that was perpetrated by another fanatical Islamist terrorist organization, al Qaeda, whose leaders are being harbored by the Taliban, the world was at least temporarily galvanized against their religious extremism. Steeled in opposition it was, and the Taliban was cracked like any hollow, empty shell can be. Now, its broken shards which can still maim the societies in which they are embedded are regrouping in a further effort to dictate conformity to their distorted beliefs. Such destructive coercion is once again being confronted by a coalition of nations and peoples as something that drags humanity back into the past as opposed to advancing it into the future.

Opposites teach and correct.

From this and a host of other examples it would appear to me that God encourages opposites to both advance His plan and to teach and correct us as necessary. When it comes to our development and enlightenment, the existence of opposing forces eventually pushes us to some reexamination, moderation, or redirection of our thoughts, systems, and actions. Apparently, that is good for us; humans advance in response to resistance. The very existence of someone saying that there can be no opposition drives humans to prove that there can be, that they can do what their opposites say they can't.

The tensions opposites and opposition create draws me to the realization that no matter how many sides there are in any given encounter, they are all pulling against a midpoint or balance position that can be found somewhere in between their positions. It is that balance point that has moved humanity forward through its history and, when tracked, charts its advances.

By and large, most of us seem to avoid that point, refusing, for as long as possible, to occupy it as the logical solution that was no doubt identified early on. Instead of working out our conflicts, we fuel them, to pointless delay in the best-case scenario or ungodly cost or loss of life in the worst case. If we follow God's lead, we will use balancing forces as fulcrums to lever mankind into a better future.

In the meantime, however, the majority of humanity continues to bicker or fight with at least one other person and believes that *I and my beliefs are better than you and yours*. But am I better than you are? Who, or what, defines better? Do I have a better education or a better job? Is my life better or are my beliefs better than the person across the room or across the world? The answer I propose to these questions is that only God is the rightful judge of "better."

We are the product of a modern incarnation of God's Tower of Babel. We're different, one from another, in education, experience, station, beliefs, lifestyles, and temperament. We may think that these attributes of our lives are better than those of others. We may even be on a crusade to convince the world that we are right. But we'd be wrong, because different is not better. It is only different.

God's truths apply to all opposites.

As the struggle goes on for the final balance point where no difference is recognized, the basic truths God has taught us and fosters in our faiths—love one another as you love yourself, thou shall not kill, do good works, and be compassionate and merciful—still apply to all opposites. Those laws exist and are observed in every corner of the world. Those who do so are a community of neighbors, no matter how wide the geographical divide that separates them.

Each human being must come to faith and spirituality, to divinity and God, in his or her own way. We must realize that even the most evolved among us are but a minute fraction of what God is and know but a fraction of all that can be known. We must all fight against the temptation to declare to the world, and the rest of the universe of other worlds if we could reach them, too, that we, and only we, know the way, the truth, and the light.

In the words of the Trappist monk Thomas Merton, found in his *Conjectures of A Guilty Bystander* on page fifty-six, we flawed humans want to believe:

> [T]hat we have the monopoly of all truth, just as our adversary of the moment has the monopoly of all error.
>
> We then convince ourselves that we cannot preserve our purity of vision and our inner security if we enter into dialogue with the enemy, for he will corrupt us with his error. We believe, finally, that truth cannot be preserved except by the destruction of the enemy—for since we have identified him with error, to destroy him is to destroy error. The adversary, of course, has exactly the same thoughts about us and exactly the same basic policy by which he defends the "truth." He has identified us with dishonesty, insensitivity, and untruth. He believes that if we are destroyed, nothing will be left but truth.

But none of us has cornered the market on truth. There isn't only one way, or even a best way, to demonstrate belief in a Supreme Being. All of us grope, often in blindness, toward understanding. All of us fail in one way or another as individuals (and does it serve any useful purpose to count how many faults someone else has? Isn't one shortcoming enough to make the case that no one should judge another's beliefs?).

Quoting again from St. Paul's *I Corinthians*,

> Our knowledge is imperfect and our prophesying is imperfect...Now we see indistinctly, as in a mirror (of polished bronze); then we shall see face to face. My knowledge is imperfect now; then I shall know even as I am known. There are in the end three things that last: faith, hope and love, and the greatest of these is love. [13:12-13]

I would add the words used by writer Mario Vargas Llosa in quoting historian and philosopher Isaiah Berlin, "This complex sum of contradictory truths...constitutes the very fabric of the human condition." For it is through the simultaneous repulsion and attraction of opposition that all opposite distinctions ultimately disappear and a common ground emerges. When that happens, faith will be rewarded, hope will be realized, and love will be all that is left.

SIX

Gain the World, or Save the Soul—
Identifying What Matters Most

Aprofessor of philosophy once demonstrated to her class what's important in life by using two large clear plastic bowls, a box of rocks, a box of small pebbles, a box of fine sand, and two cups of coffee. She took the rocks and filled one of the bowls up to the rim. Turning to the class, she asked if the bowl was full and they agreed it was. With a slight smile, the professor picked up the box of pebbles and, shaking the bowl, began pouring pebbles into the cracks and open spaces between the piled rocks until rocks and pebbles reached the bowl's rim. Once again, she asked if the bowl was full and once again the class said yes. Finally, the professor raised the box of fine sand and, still shaking the bowl, poured in an amazing amount of the stuff as it filled all the remaining nooks and crannies between the rocks and pebbles. Now the bowl was truly packed solid.

Looking at her class, the professor declared, "This bowl is you. The rocks are what's really important in your life—family, friends, co-workers and neighbors, your health. These are the things that, if were you to lose them, would leave you devastated. The pebbles represent things that matter to you but aren't vital, like your house, the exact nature of your job, or whether you get an A or a B in this course. The sand is everything else in your life."

Then, for an encore, the professor picked up the second bowl and filled it to the brim from the box of sand. On top of the sand she dropped one rock and one pebble and mashed them down. When she did, the sand began to spill out over the bowl's side. "What does this teach us?" she asked. The class remained silent with puzzled looks on their faces. "If you put the sand in first, there's almost no room left for the far more important things represented by the rocks and pebbles," the professor said. "Always check your priorities, and focus on the really important things in your life first. Pay attention to the people who are critical to your happiness. Look after your own health and play with your kids. Don't look for the approval of strangers at the sacrifice of your relations with your family and friends.

"The sand will take care of itself if you take care of the rocks and the pebbles," the professor said.

One of the students stuck his hand up and spoke when the teacher acknowledged him. "But Professor, what are the two cups of coffee for?"

Pay attention to the people who are critical to your happiness.

Laughing, the professor slowly poured both cups into the apparently full bowl of rocks, pebbles, and sand that easily absorbed the liquid. "Never forget," she said with a broad smile, "that no matter how full your life is there is always room for a couple of cups of coffee with a friend."

It's interesting to focus on the sand as a representation of the material desires and vapid social interaction that so often preoccupy us. Desiring acquisition that goes far beyond ensuring survival, wanting easy living, and seeking pleasure at every turn aren't the rocks upon which to build a life. They're grains of sand that will hasten our destruction, latter-day false idols that we worship with precious sacrifices—our relatively brief lives—until we find out that our efforts are every bit as futile as those of the Israelites who refused to listen to God were. Our lives can be as hollow as the blood offerings of yesteryear.

Material Lessons

We have lost our sense of balance. As a society, we have crossed the line that separates procurement of basic needs and excess accumulation that never seems enough to satisfy our modern gods. How many well-off people do you know who are miserable despite their material trappings? A modicum of observation reveals that their number is vast. Too often, people define their success or lack of it in terms of dollars or resumes. It's the way score is kept. People want more and more titles and money, and more things to demonstrate to people they know or are only associated with that they are successful. Another set of initials in front of or behind their names, a bigger house, flashier cars, fancier clothes, or more expensive vacations to farther and farther away places are what we use to convince ourselves as we try to convince others that we have made it. We keep telling ourselves that if we can add just one more glittering trophy to the list of the things we own or can claim on a resume, we will be content at last.

Folks confuse happiness with possessions and titles rather than equating it with values. Possessions are inanimate objects. Titles are only words. Both provide only momentary enjoyment and satisfaction, as fleeting as the life of an innocent lamb upon an altar of purification. Real happiness comes from values, how our lives and surroundings comport to those values, and how we share those values. It comes from the professor's rocks. Without values, our lives are mired in confusion and discontent no matter what we possess. With solid values, we have the opportunity to bring happiness into our existence, to gather and store the rocks that have substance and strength instead of grains of sand that blow in the wind no matter how high the pile they top. Values withstand the test of time. We carry them throughout our lives no matter where we go. They won't disappear, but we can lose them or discard them if we fill our "bowls" with the wrong material and bury our "rocks" out of sight in the sand of trifles that smothers us.

Values withstand the test of time.

Modern society has sold us on the instant gratification that possessions offer. But instant gratification, by definition, lasts only for an instant. In our quest for momentary pleasures, we end up losing that which is most important and dear in our lives—our family and friends, and our relationship with God. We find ourselves telling Him and our loved ones that we can't be with them because we have to work ever harder for the applause of others or for the things we don't really need and could never satisfy us. We lose sight of the truth that the best experiences in life come from our family and true friends. If we sacrifice those relationships through neglect or abuse while we pursue the esteem of acquaintances and of the crowd, we are trading sustenance for empty calories. Our inner selves go hungry while we feed the beast of conspicuous consumption.

What do the excesses of American life teach us? It is that rather than producing enduring happiness, they generate ever-increasing selfishness and an ever-narrowing outlook restricted to self. We want more sand, and there is precious little room for those closest to us and for God.

The real judgment takes place in a higher court.

I wonder why so few of us understand that. Perhaps it's because we have allowed material hallmarks to define us as human beings. We're afraid to judge ourselves on a moral basis and live by that judgment, and we're certainly unwilling to accept such judgment from friends or family. Just as that drunken preacher said, they should just mind their own business.

Some people believe that accumulation proves they have worth or acclaim or whatever other term for success their egos need. They think that when they've acquired enough, no one could look upon them as failures. But the judgment that really matters takes place in another, higher court where God presides. His approval is the one that counts for all, for all time. It is His love and approval that we should endeavor to claim above all else. We can't touch it or hear it roar, and it can't be measured with the exactness of a bank account. It is quiet and deep inside of us, but every bit as real as the world outside. It can be felt during moments of reflection, and it can be seen in charitable acts. Though it can't be quantified, it is the most satisfying thing in the world, and it can fill every bowl.

The Grains of Truth

I am convinced that what's important is the love in our hearts, not the sand that fills our minds. Building walls of materialism to shield us from others and separate ourselves from introspection is futile. Nothing man-made—no fortress, no edict, no contrivance—can withstand decay. Love is the only thing that lasts forever. It's the only wealth worth having because it provides without fail the happiness we look for elsewhere.

God wants us to be happy; He's made that clear throughout the Bible. But it's up to us to find it, to use our free will to make choices that lead us to it. When each of us finds it, all of us will have it. And isn't that what's really important?

Our aforementioned stubbornness, with a healthy measure of insecurity, prevents the attainment of what we really want most. In my law practice, I have noticed that many of my clients who are already rich claim to be searching for happiness, but all they seem to find is more money. The extreme form of such a search is demonstrated in the spectacle of leaders of various nations or corporations who loot their companies and national treasuries of billions of dollars for ill-conceived purposes and their own greed. Saddam Hussein, Ferdinand Marcos,

Manuel Noriega, the Russian kleptocracy, and a number of American CEOs are but a handful of the scores who come to mind.

Why steal billions? Does personal gain purchase happiness? What can one individual or family do with a billion stolen dollars? It's far more money than anyone could possibly spend on personal gratification and self-aggrandizement, and yet many try to do so and many more long for such an opportunity. It happens just because the perpetrators have the power to do the taking and cannot resist using it. This is greed run amok that devastates the lives of millions of others and proves to be futile to the thieves in the end.

You might be wondering how the despicable greed of rogue CEOs, dictators, and fallen presidents-for-life could have anything to do with ordinary folk. If we can say we would never do what Marcos, Hussein, or a CEO-run-wild did, why can't we scale that thought down to our own circumstances? Their behavior is but a reflection of humankind's mindless preoccupation with acquisition that destroys families and individual souls. I've seen individuals working feverishly to acquire more simply because they can. It's there for the grabbing and they don't know how to say no. They focus only on having more money, things, and bragging rights than the other guy or gal without any real thought as to what it does to them, their families, and society.

Build Your Life Upon Rock

I propose that rather than becoming preoccupied with our own mindless gain, we should applaud and emulate the people who, unheralded and unsung, keep our world running. They are little rewarded and often ignored, even abused, by those of us who should thank them the most. Included at the top of my personal list of such folks are mothers, teachers, and ministers. Their love and dedication is what should be honored and held above all else.

What is important is how well we live our lives and choosing to give our love, as God has taught us, to every person, near or far, we can touch. Whatever your station in life is, there are abundant opportunities to exhibit love instead of greed. Love instead of vanity. Love instead of pride. In a word, love instead of selfishness.

For me, this is exemplified by Chesterfield Smith, a man who is one of my personal heroes and, during his life, a friend. Chesterfield died just a few years ago and was a giant of his time. Though most people will not recognize the name, he has touched all of us.

Chesterfield was a lawyer's lawyer. Coming out of World War II as a highly decorated combat veteran, he built a major national law firm while emphasizing pro bono work to its attorneys. He spent countless hours mentoring the careers of minorities, women, and the otherwise disadvantaged without looking for thanks or recognition. He became president of the American Bar Association and in that capacity in 1972 he was the first to stand up and declare, in the face of President Richard Nixon's attempts to stonewall his presidential conduct relative to Watergate, that "No man is above the law." His leadership was one of the driving forces behind the Watergate investigations that changed the course of American history for the better.

Doing well by doing good.

While Chesterfield Smith touched, in hugely positive ways, many, many lives, I doubt he will be much remembered by future generations despite his being featured in Tom Brokaw's book, *The Greatest Generation*. But he had the satisfaction of knowing that he had lived up to his motto of "doing well by doing good."

The inward satisfaction that Chesterfield's kind of action engenders is our best hope for happiness and enjoyment of our lives. It's the embodiment of love. It allows us to better appreciate those possessions we do choose to keep around us, and makes the things that don't really matter less important. It provides the kind of security that millions of tons of bombs can't, regardless of the interim victories that result from their use. Will nuclear proliferation preserve the nuclear family, or hasten its destruction?

Again, nothing man-made survives very long; no man-made plans or schemes that focus on earthly gain will get us to the Promised Land. We must get past ourselves to find ourselves and the way to God's approval that differs greatly from the kind we too often seek.

Grains of Sand

As they are so important to so many of us, let's spend some more time considering human praise and condemnation. It is amazing to me how many people spend their lives chasing after the one and trying to avoid the other. But either one of them is important, if at all, only if they help us in accomplishing our real missions in life as set for us by God.

I fear that rather than reaching for God's approval and our own inner happiness that is attained by serving others, too many of us remain constantly fixated on a search for approval from strangers. That search seems to me to be central to what drives the majority of us throughout our lives, but I'm convinced that condemnation and praise are really tests for all of us and a trap for many. I've come to believe we must approach the opinions of others with great caution. They are a reflection of our motives and actions, but their true value comes when we judge them for their content and not their sound. If valid, they provide guides for improving our future conduct. If not, they will seduce us into disaster if we heed them.

Praise or adulation can be overpowering. I had a taste of that in 1988 during the Democratic Party's National Convention in Atlanta, Georgia. At its culmination, I and a number of others were on the podium with Mike Dukakis as he accepted the party's nomination for the Presidency of the United States. The image of mass adulation, seas of undulating signs and walls of sound projected towards us by a packed hall of howling delegates, adulation that rushed and rolled over me in overwhelming waves, is forever imprinted in my mind. It was something I could almost lean into and feel as if it were holding me in its grip. Even though I was only part of the window dressing for

Mike, it was beyond intoxicating. I don't know how he handled it as well as he did.

See with your inner eye.

But a trap exists for individuals with a weak foundation who seek praise and avoid condemnation without reference to whether they are deserved and what it is they are being condemned or praised for. People whose principal goals in life are public approval and acclaim will do or support anything they think the public agrees with. They will tack to any wind without regard to whether such conduct is actually in their own or society's best interest, whether it is right or wrong, whether it will result in smooth sailing or a crash upon a reef. Their focus becomes the feeding and protection of their own egos that always seem to need larger and larger doses of such empty approval.

On the other hand, individuals who select a program of action, philosophy, or course of conduct based on the common good, on what is right, and then consistently act on those choices may not receive immediate public or historic acclaim. But in the long run, they will be thanked and remembered by those we mentioned earlier who really count—their loved ones and God. During quiet moments, they will be able to smile as they look at themselves with that inner eye we all possess, knowing they have garnered the approval that has real meaning.

History's focus and God's are two different things. As an example, consider Julius Caesar and St. Timothy, two men who lived in the same historic era although not at the same time. We acknowledge Julius Caesar, a Roman general and politician, with acclaim as one of the most famous men in the history of the Western world. In stark contrast, Timothy spent his life as the companion and successor of the Apostle Paul. He receives far, far less of our notice and praise. But, fame aside, which of the two had the greatest positive impact on history and humanity's development?

History's focus differs from God's.

I think I can make a good argument for Timothy. Caesar added conquered lands to the Roman Empire, co-opted or killed Rome's more civic-minded officials, and destroyed the Roman Republic with his tyranny. His real interest was self-aggrandizement and his glorification without regard to the decades of civil war they produced both before and after his death. As a result, we know a great deal about both him and his life. Timothy, on the other hand, toiled in relative obscurity. He was dedicated to the cause of Christianity, its advancement, and the welfare of his contemporary Christians. His and Paul's work made great strides toward ensuring the survival of the Christian faith. As Timothy ministered to others, he accepted anonymity without regard to his own self-interest and worked at great personal sacrifice without complaint. We know almost nothing about him.

In the words of Ernle Bradford, one of Julius Caesar's scores of biographers, "It must be conceded that de Tocqueville's description of Napoleon is even more relevant to Caesar: 'He was as great as a man can be without morality.'" Timothy was great because of his morality, faith, and dedication to a cause other than himself. Thus, his accomplishments have stood the test of time and have, in conjunction with his fellow believers, resulted in the living faith of Christianity. For the most part, Caesar's achievements disappeared with the fall of the Roman Empire.

God works in the here and now for all of us.

Julius Caesar was a man driven by his need for power and mass approval. I get the impression that despite the unbelievable amounts of political authority and human adulation he was able to amass, lasting happiness eluded him. He was always reaching for that one more thing or conquest he dreamed would make satisfaction and fulfillment happen for him. As I've noted, we know almost nothing of Timothy. But I would be willing to bet that he was more than satisfied with God's approval and the gratitude of the people he touched daily, one at a time.

Timothy had little human acclaim in his life; Caesar had an inordinate amount. That still holds true today. But which of the two do you think God loves and approves of the most? Which will He keep with him for all eternity?

Like Caesar, many of us still fail to understand that God doesn't worry about those who refuse to listen to Him. They can achieve earthly riches and acclaim as a result of shrewd dealings or evil deeds; God has the rest of eternity to deal with them. But I'm persuaded that God works in the here and now for all of us. He reproves and chastises us when we stray, succors us in our hour of need, and rests an unseen hand on our shoulder when we please Him. He talks to us in many ways; whether we hear Him or not is the question we should ask ourselves again and again.

I have known people who are proud simply because they have risen to the top in business, the professions, or public life; they bask in the applause of those below them. I've also encountered others who are secretly ashamed because they do not believe they have achieved much because of their lack of riches, public acknowledgement, or social approval. I would suggest that what both groups are missing is that God judges each of us on how well and to what purpose we use the talent, ability, and station in life He has given us. Are they dedicated to our own shallow ends, or to the service of others?

The Prosperous Life

The true measure of success is not whether we become president or whether we have failed because we simply clean rooms. To me, it is how well or poorly we do that which God has given us to do, which often has nothing to do with the work from which we earn our daily bread.

I trust that God will not judge us on how we are treated by others. Instead, I believe He will judge us on how well we treat the rest of humanity both near to us and far away, no matter what our own circumstance in life is. This is the approval we should be seeking, not that of our fellow humans or of history. In this vein, I am convinced that God will judge our charity not by the worthiness of those we help, but by the quality of giving He finds in our hearts. The irony is, however, that our charity does more for us than it does for those we aid.

When our acts of giving are done in the right frame of mind and heart, they provide us with far more lasting happiness than the worldly benefits we bestow on the recipients of our largesse do. More often than not, the people we aid continue to be beset by the basic problems that led to their conditions. And, from my experience working with the homeless, those problems are often deep-rooted and not readily solved. But giving isn't measured by its immediate effect, by the worthiness of those in need, or by the thanks we receive. It's measured by how much closer it brings us to God.

Giving is measured by how much closer it brings us to God.

It is striking to me how many people look for perfect and unsullied poverty as acceptable objects of their charitable impulses. If the poor have faults, be it laziness, lack of personal hygiene, personality or mental disorders, stubbornness, or just plain stupidity, many people tend to see them as being undeserving of charity. Apparently, what their own fate would be if God judged them by the same standards they use in their charity never crosses their minds. They conveniently overlook that perfection does not exist in either the poor or the rest of us.

Luke's story of the ten lepers comes to mind in this regard. To paraphrase that tale, on his way up to Jerusalem, Jesus was traversing the border between Galilee and Samaria. Along the way, he was accosted by ten lepers who pleaded for his pity. Invoking his charity, they begged to be healed by him. Without asking for anything in return, Jesus fulfilled their prayers and sent them off to see the priests so that they might be declared clean once again under the Law of Moses.

As they rushed away to regain human approval and the acceptance of their societies, one of them suddenly realized the true import of what had just happened to him. He alone out of the ten returned to give thanks and praise to Jesus for his miraculous act of compassion and charity. The man was a Samaritan who did not know Jesus or his teachings, and one can almost hear Jesus' ironic laugh as he told the Samaritan that his perfect faith had been his salvation. Jesus did not withdraw his charity from the nine imperfect Jewish lepers; they remained cured, but they had missed the opportunity for a far greater salvation.

The Power of Absolution

Forgiveness, another kind of charity, also benefits oneself more than the one forgiven. With an offer of forgiveness, the injured person heals himself or herself and allows happiness to return. This is because a major component of any situation where there is a need for forgiveness is the deep-seated hurt and anger of the one who has been wronged. All too often, that anger is so corrosive that it eats at the well-being of those who harbor it. It consumes their thoughts and their lives, warping everything they do. In effect, without forgiveness, injured parties go on magnifying the injury to themselves while the perpetrator suffers far less, if at all.

I'll never forget a close friend of mine who literally made himself ill over the ungrateful conduct of his brother. This friend had struggled for years to make a go of a business. Despite how tough the times were, he brought his younger brother into the firm and, without asking for any financial investment, gave him a minority stake in its ownership. When it looked like their company might go under, the brother demanded that my friend buy him out and said he didn't give a damn about the rest of their family. Hurt beyond description, my friend somehow scraped together the money just to be rid of his brother's destructive presence. What he couldn't rid himself of, however, was his anger at his brother's ungrateful conduct, and it became an obsession that hastened the downward spiral in my friend's life. It was only when this friend was able to see the effect his brother was still having on him that he could let go, forgive him, and move on with his life to new happiness.

Forgiveness benefits oneself more than the one forgiven.

109

I think this lesson also holds true on the societal level. For example, it seems to me that in the United States of today, many African-Americans are so caught up in their race's rightful anger at the historic evils of slavery and segregation that it devours their ability to move beyond those injuries and be healed as a community. In their unforgiving despair, I'm convinced they end up enslaving themselves to the past. Even though I am not a member of their race, I would suggest that, for the sake of their community, they need to forgive these terrible wrongs, the echoes of which are still stunting generation after generation of their young people. Without embracing such forgiveness, African-Americans are injuring themselves. By contrast, South Africa, which I have visited a number of times, has at least begun to learn this lesson through its Truth and Reconciliation process. I propose that we Americans need to do the same from both sides of our black/white divide.

Without embracing forgiveness, African-Americans injure themselves.

Turning to the other side of the equation, what wrongdoers have to realize is that being forgiven does not automatically restore the forgivers' respect or love for them. When an individual, community, organization or nation wrongfully hurts others by word or deed, trust and approval are destroyed. Even when the injured give up their anger at the transgressor and forgive the transgression, the wrongdoer rightfully remains diminished in the eyes of the injured. Regaining that esteem is much harder than obtaining forgiveness. It is from this prospective that one can understand the apparent lack of trust in modern America exhibited by many of its African-American citizens.

A different kind of forgiveness is self-forgiveness. In many instances, the persons we have lost respect for is ourselves. It may be because we haven't met personal standards and goals, or it may be because we have done something wrong and the memory of the transgression torments. When that happens, we need to go through the same healing process of forgiveness. The difference is that the wrongdoer and the wronged are one and the same person, and that combination can be one of the most self-destructive forces we will ever encounter.

The first step towards effective self-forgiveness is coming to grips with the imperfection or transgression that is at the root of our need for absolution. In the words of Pogo, a classic comic strip character I grew up with, "We have met the enemy and he is us."

Forgiveness is a journey that brings us back to God's love.

When the issue is imperfection, we must take stock of whether or not our standards are so unrealistic that no ordinary and inherently flawed human could meet them. If they are, we must recognize that we are but ordinary mortals and give ourselves, and the rest of the world, a break. When we do so, we will be a lot happier and others will be thankful. On the other hand, when the issue concerns wronging another, we must acknowledge our transgression to anyone who has been hurt and ask for forgiveness. Even if such forgiveness isn't forthcoming, this is the essential first step for self-forgiveness in these cases.

We must then face up to what caused us to act in a hurtful manner, and adjust our actions, emotions, and thinking so it won't happen again. After we have focused on the root cause of our anger and disappointment, we can leave those emotions behind; self-forgiveness comes with letting go.

Let us not forget that forgiveness is a process that can take months, if not years, to accomplish. In fact, it is a journey that we have to continue until we have achieved forgiveness not only in our minds, but also in our hearts and souls as well. That journey brings us back to charity—God's charity. I'm confident that a review of either history or our lives will more than demonstrate that God bestows His charity on each and every one of us, every day, in many different ways. Part of that charity is the forgiveness He rains down on us over and over again. It doesn't matter how wretched we are—He'll heal our sores as Jesus did the lepers'. God will even forgive our lack of thanks, just as Jesus did.

So if God can forgive all of us, why can't we be as charitable and forgive those around us who are in need as well?

The challenge before us is not one of amassing acclaim or material possessions. It is to increase the number of people whose lot is improved as a result of our conscious decisions to act with a charitable heart. In the end, what matters most is helping others, especially the least of God's children, without strings attached. When we give and forgive, we do thank Him, indeed, and get closer to eternal salvation.

SEVEN

Love or Hate—
Accepting Others as They Are

Faiths have love in its broadest sense as a primary focus. It is amazing to me how much we humans talk about love, read about love, focus vast segments of our entertainment on love, long for love, and dream about it. Yet, we seldom understand what love truly is or that it should be central in all aspects of our lives.

Love is not focused on self-gratification. The use of another person in fulfillment of our desires, sexual or otherwise, does not constitute love. In its purest form, love is something within each of us that focuses on nurturing and gratifying others. It is a giving of ourselves, not a taking from others.

When it comes to love, I suspect that all of us disappoint God and our fellow humans at some point. It doesn't matter who or what we are. Even God's anointed, such as King David, falter along the way. David committed murder to gratify his own lust and he deluded himself into thinking that he was acting out of love. So we should not be surprised when even the most saintly among us stumble because of their imperfections, failings, and faults. They do so as a result of their flawed humanity. But that doesn't mean we shouldn't hold love up as an ideal or stop trying to attain it. Referring again to I Corinthians, Paul makes as profound a statement about love as has ever been penned, and it merits inclusion in its entirety:

> Now I will show you the way which surpasses all the others.
>
> If I speak with human tongues and angelic as well, but do not have love, I am a noisy gong, a clanging cymbal.
>
> If I have the gift of prophecy and, with full knowledge, comprehend all mysteries, if I have faith great enough to move mountains, but have not love, I am nothing.
>
> If I give everything I have to feed the poor and hand over my body to be burned, but have not love, I gain nothing.
>
> Love is patient; love is kind. Love is not jealous, it does not put on airs, it is not snobbish.
>
> Love is never rude, it is not self-seeking, it is not prone to anger; neither does it brood over injuries.
>
> Love does not rejoice in what is wrong but rejoices with the truth.
>
> There is no limit to love's forbearance, to its trust, its hope, its power to endure.
>
> Love never fails. Prophecies will cease, tongues will be silent, knowledge will pass away.
>
> Our knowledge is imperfect and our prophesying is imperfect.
>
> When the perfect comes, the imperfect will pass away.

When I was a child I used to talk like a child, think like a child, reason like a child. When I became a man I put childish ways aside.

Now we see indistinctly, as in a mirror; then we shall see face to face. My knowledge is imperfect now; then I shall know even as I am known.

There are in the end three things that last; faith, hope and love, and the greatest of these is love. [13:1-13]

People are prone to think of what Paul wrote as defining the love between two people, but it was also meant to define the love that represents and helps us to understand God in His perfect and unlimited sense. It is the capacity to love all as we love ourselves and the ones closest to us on Earth. God's love encompasses all. It is the ideal and Paul's words describing it should come to mind more than love songs and perfect sonnets do. We must never forget God's love for all and that His every act is intended to help us. Whether those actions are directed at us as individuals or at humankind as a whole, they all come from His deep abiding love for us and all future generations.

God's acts, however, include both positive and negative components because God determines what is good for us as individuals, what is best for humankind as a whole, and what is right for all life to come. We must learn to accept the reality that we might not like a given personal circumstance that results from His broader expression of love.

God loves us enough to give us the opportunity to embrace His love. He wants us to exercise our free will and choose to exhibit His love to everyone, no matter what challenges we face. He wants us to expand the love we have that comes closest to His—the one for spouse and children—to the world at large. Instead of showing contempt for one group or another as each of us is prone to do, treating them as the lepers of yore were treated, we should express love in its purest form of all. Labels such as "obnoxious," "primitive," "misguided," or "enemy" are excuses we fall back on to justify the withholding of love. It is when we open our hearts to those we detest, however, that we are closest to the love God is.

God has commanded us to love one another as He loves us. It occurs to me that we often just don't seem to know how to do that. We hear His Golden Rule, "Do unto others as you would have them do unto you" without truly understanding it in our hearts. More often than not, we define and limit "others" to those we are comfortable with, who look like us, or think like us. And it seems that when we are willing to do unto those others in the proper way, we do so only if it doesn't hurt ourselves too much or too long in the process. A substantial number of us forgets that "others" includes God himself. We want God to be good to us, but how many are truly willing to be good back to Him by being good to the rest of His people? Not wanting to share God's bounty with the billions of people He has spread across the face of this Earth is the norm rather than the exception.

How to Love

Everything we have and are is a gift from God. He planted each of us here in this life to grow in the use of His God-given talents and opportunities, and just because we have taken advantage of these gifts does not mean that we are the sole and unique authors and proprietors of the results. Our blessings are the fruits of His love for us that we, in turn, must share with our fellow human beings wherever and whenever we encounter them, no matter their circumstances. Love isn't selective or prejudiced. It isn't something that can be turned on or off as everything else in our digital age seems to be.

We must expand our understanding of what "do unto others" represents. It doesn't only mean to give or be kind to our next-door neighbor or to those poor people on the edge of town; it must encompass those who do not share a geographical area or culture with us. It doesn't mean giving in the way that is most convenient; it means looking at others and seeing them as they truly are, not as we have prejudged them to be. It also means listening to what others have to say before we demand they listen to us; to learn from them if we want them to learn from us.

God's love encompasses all.

Love must be given without condition or expectation. I've come to understand that we cannot dictate the terms of how we love and how others will love us, no matter how much we might want to. Love, like life, is a gift, not a contract. I've found that love is destroyed or warped into something ugly when its giver proffers it with a caveat such as, "If you love me you will…" or "If God loves me, He will…" I have observed that when we do that and the one we love does not return it in the prescribed manner, more often than not we are offended. In response, we often withhold love as punishment for the failure of those who don't live up to the "contract" that has unilaterally been imposed on them. With this, we begin what becomes an endless cycle. destroying love in the process.

I'd suggest that if we cannot accept the limitations of another in giving or receiving love, we need to rethink the overall relationship before we think about administering the punishment of withholding love. If our love is not returned in the way we anticipated, we must be content with the thought that it is growing nonetheless. Just as God still loves us despite our shortcomings, we must accept the shortcomings of others who need our love.

Again, love is a gift, not a cold, hard bargain. We can't dictate the terms of such a gift. It must be freely given and freely accepted. If we give love without pre-conditions, it will be returned by its recipient as best as he or she is able to. We should be grateful for the love we get regardless of its scope; when we refuse to accept love in the manner it was given, we lose an opportunity to nurture and spread it. In a sense, we become that unfertile ground where a seed cannot take root. This does not means that we must simply accept the faults and defects of those we love who love us in return; we can and should try to help them grow and improve themselves, just as they and God help us to do. Help should be offered without a threat of withheld love if they fail us.

We can become fertile ground for the seed of love.

"The imperfect will pass away" were Paul's words. If we're conscious of the ways in which our love is flawed, we can become that fertile ground for the seed of love that God planted in our hearts. God's love has no limits; let us manifest His love by nurturing those around us, by bearing disappointment in others, and by giving without measure or expectation.

Love's Opposition

There are two sides to most things, and any discussion about love must deal with its opposite, hate. Love is an emotion of joy. It builds and uplifts. Hate is anger that leads to destruction, and self is what is all too often destroyed. Hate can obliterate in an instant that which it takes a lifetime to build—relationships, communities, and entire nations. Hate in any of its numerous forms is something we have to handle with great care. This is especially true with issues related to bigotry.

In confronting our own hatreds, the first thing we have to do is separate in our minds why we hate from what we hate. For example, it is one thing to hate a concept or conduct like evil, prejudice, or racial oppression. It is altogether something else to hate individuals, groups, or societies. We all understand why we abhor certain types of conduct. Murder, sexual abuse of children, and physical battery of the weak (to name just a few of the obvious choices) are more than wrong. The harm they produce imposes a terrible toll. We say we hate them and we do, as we should. The anger they generate in us fuels our efforts to combat these awful acts and their effects.

But that form of anger and hate is substantially different from hatred of individuals and peoples. Hate-based bigotry is an ugly thing that fuels conflicts such as the four-hundred-year-old confrontation between Catholics and Protestants in what is now Northern Ireland, and the ongoing one between whites and blacks. What leaps into my mind is what hate does on both sides of a divide. Often, this hate turns inward and becomes a way of life one expresses to those on one's own side of the fence. One approaches everyone and everything with hate as a basis for being instead of love. As a result, one is diminished as a human being, and humanity as a whole is not unaffected. The abhorrence of other people seems to come easily to us and that's a sad state of affairs. The minute someone fears another individual or group, hate is an instinctive response. Even in cases where one's life is threatened, hate comes with a heavy price.

If you ever had the chance to be personally close to someone who had been a combat infantryman, you'd know what I mean. Such combatants quite often develop an absolute, if only temporary, hatred for their enemy. They justify their battle rage and the taking of life with the fear that demonizes the enemy, reducing them to something less than human beings. On the other hand, in my experience it is quite common for combat pilots to think of an enemy aircraft as a machine they are destroying without reference to the flyers inside it, or to focus on the buildings or ground-based hardware they are bombing instead of the living people associated with those targets. The difference is that one is the hatred of people while the other is a hatred of things. The first leaves many more emotional scars than the latter because we find it far easier to separate ourselves emotionally from the hatred of things than of people.

Hate can obliterate in an instant that which took a lifetime to build.

Unfortunately, outside of combat, many folks hide behind a claim of hating a thing to justify what they are doing to people, even when what is being done to these humans is shameful. Because of fear, people hide from that shame and look for excuses to convince themselves that their actions aren't all that bad or are demanded by situational necessity. This hatred of people takes over an individual and owns him or her. It becomes who they are at their very core and it produces the Ku Klux Klans, Hitlers, and Bin Ladens of the world. It produces fanatics who base their beliefs on fear and loathing.

When we are faced with these fears, we should remind ourselves of the Apostle John's words:

Love has no room for fear; rather, perfect love casts out all fear.

And since fear has to do with punishment, love is not yet perfect in one who is afraid....

If anyone says, "My love is fixed on God," yet hates his brother, he is a liar.

One who has no love for the brother he has seen cannot love the God he has not seen.

The commandment we have from him is this: whoever loves God must also love his brother. [First Epistle of John 5:20-21]

The question, I think, then becomes who is our brother. In answer, I'd suggest that God would have us realize that it is every other person in this world. I feel He was trying to teach us this through, among other things, the parable of the Good Samaritan that Jesus used to exemplify love. Today, however, many people adore that story without accepting its true meaning.

The parable involves a Samaritan merchant on his way to Jericho who comes across a Jewish traveler crumpled in the road. The poor man had been beaten by bandits, robbed, and left there to die. Several Jews of high rank had already detoured around the victim, fearing he was dead. They did not want to risk becoming ritually impure by touching his body to find out if he was alive because, if he were dead, under the Law of Moses they would become unclean until they were again ritually purified. Even though there was deep enmity between Jews and Samaritans, the merchant stopped, tended to the man's wounds, and took him to a wayside inn where he paid for the Jew's care.

In the Palestine of Jesus' time, Samaritans were despised by Jews. They were a foreign people who had been planted by the Assyrians, in the part of the old northern kingdom of Israel that came to be known as Samaria, to replace the exiled Israelites languishing in Damascus or Babylonia. Once settled there, the Samaritans had adopted what the Jews saw as a corrupt and debased form of Judaism. This Samaritan worship of God, as well as the Samaritans themselves, became anathema to any devout Jew. For Jesus to say via a parable that Samaritans could be as good as or even better than Jews was, in his time, both offensive and revolutionary. However, it was his way of teaching how far the concept of recognizing those you despise as your brother should go. Based on this story, I believe God wants us to view the rest of humanity as Good Samaritans.

Why do we embrace the opposite of what we want in our own lives?

I have observed that there is a natural inclination among humans to want love, and to become depressed when it isn't received. So I ask myself, why do so many of us spend inordinate amounts of time and energy teaching ourselves and those around us to hate, when what we want for ourselves is love? Why do we embrace the opposite of what we want in our own lives?

We humans have perfected the art of being against; we come together in opposition with a moment's notice. We have summoned the bravery and have mastered the skills necessary to face death and kill others in combat. I feel we must also summon an equal courage to love in every circumstance. That is what seems to elude us and, again, I wondered why. Is it because we find it more convenient to be against something and to hate the people associated with it than it is to stand for something based on the love we have to give to others? Even when hate is justified, it is empty if it isn't ultimately replaced with its opposite. Most of the world opposed communism, apartheid, and Taliban rule in Afghanistan. But after those three ideologies collapsed in the face of our opposition, we weren't very good at planting something better. We didn't gather our love to do the expensive, slow work of building up the societies that sat devastated in the wake of what we opposed. Instead, we left the masses to their ruins and went back to thinking about ourselves. Rather than seizing an opportunity to spread love, we left a vacuum where hate had a chance to thrive again.

Hate exists because we choose to exhibit or tolerate it. It will live on until our love is powerful enough to vanquish it once and for all.

Connecting with Others

At some point in our lives, we are, in one way or another, preoccupied with sex—to have it or not, wanting and needing sex, afraid of it, frustrated by it, in love with it, obsessed with it, or confused by it. That's not a bad thing, necessarily. Sexual gratification is one of the few pleasures that are available to the majority of the world's population, and I'd warrant that it's safe to say almost all of the six-plus billion souls inhabiting Earth today didn't get here as the result of intellectual pursuits. But many of us spend an inordinate amount of time focused on sexual gratification. We long for "fulfillment" and often look for what our fantasies tell us will be the perfect sexual experience. As it is with drug and other addictions, this yearning becomes number one in a personal pantheon of concerns.

The result is that people expend vast amounts of effort, energy, and money either searching for sex, indulging in it, or trying to control or suppress it. In country after country, I have observed that the media are filled with discussions and representations of whether and how we enjoy our sex lives: Are we bored with them, is there something missing in them, can they be enhanced? At the same time, the pulpits of churches, temples, and mosques ring with denunciations of the subject and some countries try to submerge any written or pictorial reference to sexual relations. Both of these fixations miss the point, however. If the only concern is a need for gratification and pleasure or the suppression of a natural impulse, the partnering opportunity that sex was intended by God to be is lost. In its highest expression, sexual relations involve two feeling, sharing people.

Instead of focusing on suppression or what we take from our sexual partner, it seems to me that God wants us to approach sex as an opportunity to give of ourselves to a partner. Such sharing should not be just a mask to manipulate a greater return for self. Sex can be a marvelous and primary avenue for an individual to learn about and practice putting another human being's needs before one's own. In that context, loving pleasure is reflected back to us and magnified many times over. Our reward then is not just physical gratification; heightened communication and intimacy are the outcome. This more important connection on a primary, spiritual level is the start of the broader connection God wants us to likewise share outside of the sexual realm with all of His children.

When we abuse the gifts God provided, we violate His plan.

I believe God made sex wonderful and pleasurable to ensure that we engage in it. Why? First, it was and is without a doubt the best way to guarantee the survival of our species. This tells us that God clearly wants humanity and the rest of life to continue onward into the future. Second, I believe He also wants us to use it as an opportunity to learn to control our individual desires and appetites, focusing instead on lovingly benefiting someone else. At the same time, it is an opportunity to exercise our intellect by finding ways to ethically limit our numbers so those whom we bring into the world can function above a primal level and focus on the improvement of humanity as a whole.

In this light, we can trust that the enjoyment of sex is not evil in and of itself. I believe God intended it to be used to foster love, and I am confident that is also true for all of our other legitimate appetites. For example, we do not say that it is somehow wrong or evil to savor the act of dining with others and enjoying the tastes of good food. Jesus himself loved to eat and delighted in the company of others at table. He noted that he had been accused of being a glutton for doing so, but he did it anyway. However, with each pleasure available to us there is the parallel temptation to become caught up in its ever-increasing indulgence. At some point, that indulgence becomes destructive, and I would argue that when we let pleasure control us, we pervert God's intentions and drive ourselves further from others and Him. When we abuse or become addicted to the gifts God provided, we violate His plan.

Addictions are not limited just to individuals.

To me, temptations are like a downhill walk from home. Going away is always easy; coming back up is hard work. The greater the temptation, the steeper the incline, and the harder it is to get back home.

Contrary to what many might think, addictions are not always obvious. An ever- increasing need to habitually fulfill a particular desire is accepted by many without recognition of its harmful potential as an unrecognized addiction. Addictions are not limited just to individuals, either. They can be humanity-wide in nature and can lead to mass defilement or destruction. Among these addictions is a compulsion for rampant procreation. Year in and year out, consumed by economic needs at the family level, or by nationalistic desires for human fodder on the political level, or by religious edicts on a societal one, we pile human on human and strain the Earth's resources. Too many of us are still blind to the catastrophically destructive implications of the resulting overpopulation. It's impossible for me to imagine anyone making a legitimate argument that our self-destruction is what our loving God wants for us. Instead, I trust that what He does want is for us to come to grips with all of our addictions, including that of indiscriminate reproduction.

An Intimate Lesson

I'm confident God gave us sexual pleasure because He wants us to learn to express love and caring in all of their forms to others, especially our most intimate partner, in the same way as we love and care for ourselves. It is only logical that He did not intend us to use these pleasures to harm or threaten any individual or humankind as a whole. We need to heed God's admonition to love our neighbors all across this world. I would argue that means facing up to the worldwide economic imbalances that force impoverished families into producing large numbers of children as a form of social security to ensure survival. Where there are too many mouths to feed and too many souls who can't be reached as a result because they are consumed with primal needs, God's plans for broader unity and human growth are thwarted.

The drive for sexual gratification isn't going to go away. I believe we must provide worldwide family planning and safe sexual contraception to limit our numbers without forcing God into doing it for us by using modern-day "Horsemen of the Apocalypse"—pollution, disease, war, and famine. I fear that use them He will, however, if we give Him no other choice. One way or another, He'll get us to listen to what He has to say and to use our intellect and free will as they are supposed to be used.

We cannot presume that God's love for all of humanity will prevent the consequences of our selfish pursuits. Addiction in any form consumes those who choose to do something now at the expense of what follows. I don't doubt that if God has to drive us, as He did the Israelites, into a modern-day equivalent of the wilderness to ensure the survival of a core of humanity that executes His will, then that is what He will do. We must choose a different scenario by tempering our pleasures with a greater good that everyone can share, and thus conquer the challenge of intimacy.

Many view non-traditional sexual relationships as a personal threat.

That challenge includes our attitudes towards same-sex relations. Homophobia is widespread throughout the world. The people who are horrified by the thought of male-on-male or female-on-female sex cannot be counted, and many view non-traditional sexual relations as a personal threat.

I must confess that I suffered from that prejudice at one point in my life. When I attended the U.S. Naval Academy in the late 1950s and early 1960s, homophobia was drummed into me. Homosexuality was a punishable offense under the Uniform Code of Military Justice; even a suspicion of homosexuality would get someone thrown out of the Academy in a heartbeat. Several of my classmates weren't seen again after they'd been spotted in the wrong bars. No explanation was ever offered to justify their disappearance, but it didn't take an Einstein to figure out what happened. None of the rest of us wanted to get kicked out or be thought of as "pantywaists," so we despised and shunned gays and everything associated with their lifestyle. Having absorbed that belief while at the Academy, I carried it with me on my initial fleet postings.

In February, 1962, I was forced to rethink my position, though. The destroyer I was on was headed back to the States after a six-month deployment in the Mediterranean. We got caught up in a monstrous winter storm that hampered our progress across the Atlantic Ocean. About halfway home, all the destroyers in our carrier task force ran low on fuel, and we had to execute an underway refueling from a tanker in a ferocious gale that would buffet both vessels. My ship was selected to make the first attempt at a hookup that would pump the fuel we had to have.

Homophobia is deeply rooted in the Old Testament.

I was in charge of a dozen sailors and responsible for the ship's forward refueling station one level above the main deck, just aft of a five-inch gun mount. Despite frigid temperatures and huge seas crashing onto our decks, we made it alongside the tanker and got the refueling hoses over from it as our two ships rolled and pitched like bucking broncos. As they did so, the two vessels corkscrewed towards each other and everyone held his breath in fear of a collision. Though we had only been able to take on a small amount of the needed fuel, it got so bad that the ships' captains decided to abandon the attempt, clear the decks of all personnel, and break away. When the emergency order came from the bridge to get all my people off the open deck and under cover, we temporarily secured the refueling gear and hustled below.

After we pulled clear of the tanker, the equipment had to be retrieved and I called for volunteers to go out on deck with me to get it. Only one of the dozen drenched and frozen men stepped forward, a seaman all of us were convinced was gay. He and I went back out into the storm to the ship's forward level and, despite being swept off our feet several times by seas that crashed over the foredeck, we recovered what we needed to and made it back under cover. From that point on, I knew that I had to change my attitude about a group that I had felt was beneath me and had despised.

Just because something is drummed into us doesn't mean it shouldn't be questioned.

I came to understand that my change of perception about gays was part of the process of learning about something that I had been struggling with since I was a young boy. Just because a concept or belief had been drummed into me by someone or something I loved or admired did not mean I shouldn't question it. I didn't have to go on blindly believing something that I knew was wrong. Of equal importance to me was the realization that I didn't have to stop loving or admiring the flawed people or institutions whose teaching had been erroneous.

Homophobia is deeply rooted in the Old Testament prohibitions against same-gender sex that were repeated in St. Paul's letters. For argument's sake, let's accept for the moment that homosexuality is a Biblical sin under the Laws of Moses, and that gays are thus damned for a mortal transgression against that particular law. If we do that, however, we can't ignore the fact that if we apply such Mosaic standards across the board, we are all damned as well—every human has surely sinned against one of those Laws in one way or another, at one time or another.

Proscribing homosexuality no longer serves any worthwhile purpose.

Thus, homosexuality is but another example of how none of us is better than anyone else. Most of us might even be considered worse than homosexuals if we broke a law as a result of a conscious choice. For I do not believe that most homosexuals elect his or her sexual identity anymore than the rest of us selected ours. Given society's attitudes towards homosexuality, it is a path fraught with pain and rejection; who would opt for homosexuality if a genetic makeup didn't compel him or her in that direction?

Too many of us conveniently forget or ignore Paul's message that Jesus wanted to free us from eternal damnation under the Mosaic Law's impossibly harsh directives because humans could not meet their standard of compliance. So, if God could forgive King David's mortal sin of murdering the Hittite Uriah to cover up his adultery with Uriah's wife, Bathsheba, why can't humans forgive the Biblical sin of homosexuality? And isn't this just another example of a law that should be changed?

If we take an honest look into our hearts, I'm confident that we will find some sin that requires forgiveness. I suspect that will be so until the end of days. Most of us forgive our own sins and the others we encounter in the rest of our fellow men on a daily basis; why not that one? Homosexuals are God's children, too, and are entitled to acceptance, forgiveness, and salvation. They do not reproduce themselves, but they exist nonetheless because God wants them to exist.

Salvation cannot be attained at the expense of another individual or group.

God makes the genetic choice of sexual orientation for each of us; the majority happens to be heterosexual, but that doesn't mean the homosexual, bisexual, and transsexual minorities are any less in His eyes. Why should they be so in ours? If non-heterosexuals conform to the rest of society's laws and norms, what right do we have to cast the first stone? I would argue that any law condemning homosexuality is one that God would now have us change. When the Bible's prohibitions against homosexuality were handed down to the Israelites thousands of years ago, God wanted the Jews and the rest of humanity to increase their numbers in an under-populated world where life was tenuous. At that time, such non-heterosexual conduct threatened the survival of both the

Israelites and the human race. But the threat of extinction associated with non-procreation no longer exists. Proscribing homosexuality as a social or religious taboo no longer serves any worthwhile purpose; all that it does now is create more opportunities to exhibit hate instead of love.

We do not have to applaud homosexuality or advocate that others adopt it. But we do have to acknowledge non-heterosexuals as neighbors. We must not fall into the trap that has many disguises, the one that suggests salvation can be attained at the expense of another individual or group. That mindset didn't work in ancient Egypt or Nazi Germany or anywhere else it was tried, and it won't work for self-righteous arbiters of sexual conduct, either. Even if all non-heterosexuals disappear as the Naval Academy Midshipmen of my youth did, the stain of our personal sins would remain.

Instead of looking for groups of neighbors to damn, mastery of self is the challenge God sets before us. The flaws inherent in each of us are enough to keep us occupied; worrying about another's sexual orientation should be far down on everyone's list of priorities. Let us hope that God does not judge us as harshly as we are prone to judge others, but if we seek intimacy more than physical gratification and connect with others on a deeper level, the hope for a connection with God will be realized.

EIGHT

Live for Today, or for Eternity— Sinning No More

I n contemplating the potential consequences of God's judgment at the moment of our exit from life here on Earth, I would suggest we consider the question of how many of us fear death and long for youthful immortality on Earth. I would guess the correct answer to that one would be: the vast majority of us.

Intellectually, we all understand the approaching and inevitable cessation of our body's capacity to sustain our corporal existence. But what is our understanding of immortality? When we dream of that word, do we want an eternal existence here in this world, or in Heaven? I suspect most of us would like to continue on indefinitely as the imperfect beings we are. If we are honest, we'd admit that we would prefer the young, vigorous version of ourselves to continue living in this world forever. Alas, that is not to be.

In II Corinthians 5:1, Paul refers to our bodies as "the earthy tents in which we dwell." Those "tents" fray and become careworn over the years. People are prone to forget that the beauty of youth is, as youth itself is, only transitory. It must fade at some point just as a flower does. It is, at best, a temporary beauty that is given to us by God rather than achieved by any merit of our own. It should be enjoyed like a season of the year. And yet, earthly immortality is what many of us long for. When I think of that longing, I am reminded of the wry comment of a young lady I dated more years ago than I like to acknowledge: "Women, if given the choice, would choose physical beauty over brains because most men can see better than they can think." Fortunately, she added to my chagrin, the choice is not ours to make.

Many of us long for earthly immortality.

None of us is going to achieve corporal immortality, however; we'll all be ashes some day. So if God grants us Heaven, how would we, as flawed and imperfect as we are in our current incarnations, spend that eternity? In replying to this question, I can just imagine the vast majority of us waving our hands and exclaiming, "We've been told God's going to make us perfect so we can perfectly enjoy His perfect Heaven for all time. That's what's going to happen, isn't it?" My response would be, "I'm not so sure about that." Based on my layman's biblical studies and theology, I cannot find this as a direct promise in the Bible. You can infer it, more or less, from certain passages, but it is not all that clear.

In Romans 2:7 and I Corinthians 15:53-54, Paul tells us we will have eternal life and be incorruptible. That, however, is not the same as perfect, is it? Jesus' response to the Sadducees in Mark 12:18-25 when they tried to trap him with the conundrum of the seven brothers all married to the same wife addresses the issue of life after death, but it doesn't clarify the notion of perfection, either. Jesus said that we shall all "live like angels in heaven." But we Christians know that angels can be imperfect, too. We believe that Satan and his minions are fallen angels who were imperfect in their love for God and acceptance of His rule. Instead, they grew envious of God and sought equality with Him. They could not spend eternity simply enjoying Heaven and serving under God as He commanded. So, if angels aren't perfect, I wonder what makes us think that we will be when and if we get to Heaven?

Use your time wisely.

So how might the imperfect humans we are spend eternity? To find the answer, it is instructive to look at how we spend the time God has given us here on Earth. First, we work to support ourselves and our families. But my understanding of Heaven is that there would be no corporal needs of any kind there; we won't have to worry about starving to death or keeping a roof over our heads. Then, what do most people do when they are not working? It seems to me that by and large they waste time; they kill it. Folks watch television, fascinated or bored by endless numbers of mindless shows that semi-entertain them at best. They listen to radios and go to movies so they won't have to think. Many eat, take up hobbies, or follow sports just to pass the time. Or they simply do nothing of substance as they wait for the minutes, hours, and days to tick by. Is that what they want to do for all eternity?

Certainly, there is nothing wrong with doing things that are truly enjoyable or enrich our lives and those of others in some way. But it seems to me that far too much of what we do in the name of enjoyment is merely meant to make time go by as we seek to ignore the rest of the world, with all its problems, parked right outside our doors, and our own problems, buried deep inside, not to be disturbed. After all, our time is too short to be bothered, right?

Choose to foster the soul.

But eternity is endless and that is something we have to keep in mind in considering Jesus' resurrection. It has symbolic meaning for us mortals and teaches us that God has created a way to defeat the deaths of our not-so-important physical shells, these "tents in which we dwell." Even if these houses, so to speak, burn down, our real lives—our souls—will still go on.

We have to get ourselves into shape to weather God's eternity because I cannot imagine He intends us to spend it imitating vegetables or herds of mindlessly grazing cattle. God gives us the opportunity to live our lives to the fullest, to be enriched by both physical and spiritual connections. We should use as many of the minutes we are allotted here on Earth that aren't needed to meet basic survival needs to tap the sacred consciousness that's all around us. We should choose to foster the soul.

When we focus on passive entertainment and meaningless pastimes, we waste one of the most precious earthly things we possess—the ticks on our life clocks. If we would take just half of the time we expend without joy or spiritual profit in shallow pursuits and utilized that time for something on a broader scale, such as helping others, reading, thinking, or simply talking to one another, I'm confident our lives would be much richer and more meaningful. I think we would also find that we were learning; learning about life, ourselves and our neighbors who inhabit this wonderful world with us. In doing that, we'll learn about God, too. Ongoing learning, I would argue, is critical because I have come to believe that when you stop learning, you start dying.

We can better the world by bettering ourselves.

Nonetheless, many of us do not want to learn about the world because we don't want to be challenged to do something to make it better. We want to shield ourselves from others' burdens as we try to shield ourselves from sickness and death. But, despite the longing for "just a little more time," the "Master of the House" comes to call sooner or later. Mortality is God's way of teaching us how we should live now so we can live for all eternity. We can choose to fritter away the hours we have, or use at least some of them for a greater good. We can choose to better the world by bettering ourselves. Without renewal through death and birth, humanity would remain mired in its imperfections, never growing or improving.

With that in mind, I've pondered whether our souls are reborn in a physical form until they achieve perfection on Earth.

Rebirth

Christians have been taught that we are damned for eternity if we end our lives without God's forgiveness. This presupposes that life is a one-shot deal; you either get it right, here and now, or you've blown your only chance at salvation—your soul is doomed to Hell forever. It occurred to me, however, that God wouldn't do that. Isn't it probable that, as magnanimous and compassionate as He has proved Himself to be in dealing with humanity here on Earth, He would be equally loving in dealing with us in the hereafter and give us another chance to get things right? Put another way, it seems most illogical that the God who offers us multiple chances at redemption during our short corporal lives would punish souls for all eternity when that punishment cannot lead to change and salvation. And yet Christians are taught that rebirth or redemption of those already dead and damned are not part of their faith; the concept of reincarnation is thought to be found only in the Eastern religions. But that may not be so.

Paul declares in I Corinthians 5:5, in reference to an unnamed man who had been embroiled in an incestuous relationship with his step-mother, that "I hand him over to Satan for the destruction of his flesh, so that his sprit may be saved on the day of the Lord." This suggests a second chance after corporal death. Also, the Jews of Christ's time believed in prior lives for themselves and others. This is demonstrated by the New Testament story of the man born blind:

As (Jesus) walked along he saw a man who had been blind from birth.

> His disciples asked him, "Rabbi, was it his sin or that of his parents that caused him to be born blind?"
>
> "Neither," answered Jesus. "It was no sin, either of this man or of his parents. Rather, it was to let God's works show forth in him." [John 9:1-3]

Taking pity on the man, Jesus worked on the Sabbath and restored his sight. When the Pharisees learned of this they were incensed at Jesus' violation of Moses' prohibition against laboring on God's holy day. Adding insult to their "injury," the cured man had the temerity to defend Jesus to their faces. The Pharisees attacked the poor fellow with vehemence and declared, "What!...You are steeped in sin from your birth and you are giving us lectures?" [John 9:34] That was just what Jesus' disciples had assumed when they asked him about what sins had caused the man to be born blind.

With Jesus' response to his disciples in mind, I conclude that a baby could not have already committed a sin in this life at the moment he or she is born. To further support that belief, we need only turn to Romans 9:10-11 where, in reference to Jacob and Esau, Paul writes, "...they were yet unborn and had done neither good nor evil." The way I see it, any sin horrendous enough to be punishable by blindness at birth would have had to occur in another life.

From the above it would seem Jesus, his disciples, and the Pharisees might have believed in the concept of prior lives and reincarnation. There is ample additional historical evidence that reincarnation was a belief extant among ancient Jews. As I understand it, today's Ultra-Orthodox Hasidic Jews view transmigration and reincarnation as an opportunity for sinful souls who committed wrongs in their prior lives to atone for a previous life's sins. Much of modern Judaism seems to have abandoned the concept, perhaps in response to Christian teachings surrounding the question of resurrection.

Today, as part of our Resurrection Faith, Christians believe in at least one return to earthly form for each of us—at God's final judgment of all humanity. It is a scene that has been portrayed down through the ages: all of us will be brought back to life to participate with the then-living in our ultimate universal judgment. This appears to be a form of reincarnation or rebirth that Christians may not recognize as such.

As God relegates us to either Heaven or Hell at the moment of our corporal deaths, there should be no need for a second sentencing at that future final judgment, absent some other consideration. Thus, if

God judges us once, but plans to reincarnate us to face a final judgment along with those who are then among the living, why wouldn't He demonstrate His love by doing so at other times? Reincarnation could be the ultimate example of His forgiveness, an opportunity for us to better apply His lessons and avoid eternal damnation. I suspect this issue is one of those that will become clearer down the road when our body of knowledge increases sufficiently.

Avoiding Eternal Damnation

It is worthwhile to consider that Hell might not be just an abstraction. The Bible tells us that God does chastise those He loves, and our suffering today is no doubt part of His plan. So, as others have suggested, Hell could be what humanity has created here on Earth. We are surrounded by poverty, greed, degradation, exploitation, sadism, sadness, fear, envy, misery, anxiety, pain, injury, sickness, hunger, war, and death. With the partial exceptions related to injury, sickness, pain, and death, all of these are caused by us humans. It can thus be argued that we, in effect, make our own hells; there is no need for God to create one for us. If we couple this with the concept of rebirth, maybe God wants to give us a chance to do better until we eradicate all the aspects of life that engender hell on Earth. It may be we are destined to exist in hell until we live as God intends us to.

When we consider that possibility, a course of action presents itself. If it is true, we have a stake in a future beyond our present lifetimes and we could change today to have a better tomorrow. However, Winston Churchill's comment that "Men (and women) occasionally stumble over the truth, but most of them quickly pick themselves up and hurry off as if nothing ever happened" reminds us that knowing something doesn't mean we'll do something about it. As we "hurry off" to other pursuits, it appears to me that we are all too often chasing fantasies of our own private heavens here on Earth that exclude everyone but the tiny immediate circles of like-minded people we already know. We can't or won't perceive the needs of those who are beyond our immediate fields of concern. We haven't learned that others mark the path to Heaven; we fail to understand that such limited thinking creates, spreads, and perpetuates hell on Earth.

Others mark the path to Heaven.

We must focus on what Paul refers to in Colossians 1:16 as "Powers and Principalities"—the societal, political, and religious structures necessary for humanity's ongoing existence and growth. He suggested that nations, governments, and hierarchical religious organizations had fallen from grace, and a casual survey of those institutions today would suggest that this is still so. Greed, insecurities, and thirst for power have allowed man-made structures, our latter-day Towers of Babel, to master us. If we are going to transform our earthly hell into something better, we must speak with the common language of love that pervades man's creations when they are used best to service all of humanity's needs. If we stop building monuments that don't endure and live according to God's plan, every moment of our lives will be a sacrament instead of the sacrilege that too many of them are now. Salvation will be more than a hope.

We must speak with the common language of love.

Regardless of the number of incarnations we have, the way we lived will be judged by God and I am convinced it is the content of that judgment that we must be concerned about. I thought about that a while back as I was attending the funeral of a friend's elderly mother. She had been brought up on a farm and was an unpretentious woman whose principal occupation was the raising of her own children and providing bountiful love, care, guidance, and a good example to those around her. She was probably not a great intellect, and her son told me that her name had never appeared in a newspaper until they printed her minor obituary. In listening to this woman's young minister struggle just a bit to talk about such a plain, simple person, an equally simple truth occurred to me: God judges us by the quality of the lives we have led, not by our mental brilliance, accomplishments, accumulation, or public acclaim. I suspect our achievements could tower as mountains do and they might still amount to nothing before God. For if, in His judgment, the most worthy parts of our lives—love, honesty, and care of others—do not meet the standard of that otherwise unremarkable woman, I'm convinced we will be guilty in His eyes. Salvation will be beyond our grasp.

That is part of what Paul was trying to teach us in I Corinthians 13 to which I've referred. For me, that is also the message at the core of much of his other writings. As I pondered the thought of individual judgment, I thought, too, about the nature of God's judgment of humanity in general. What is it that He really wants from us as a whole? The writings of the prophets and psalmists seem to tell us that He does not need our worship, and yet He has facilitated many religions and cultures that dictate how that should be done and what the consequences of non-conformance are.

I have been told by more than one Christian that unless people accept Jesus Christ as their Savior, they cannot hope for God's final salvation. Those who haven't will spend eternity in either purgatory or hell, no matter how loving, upright, charitable, and righteous their lives were here on Earth because God so decreed. That is not what those who spoke for God in the Bible were trying to teach us, though. Consider, for example, Paul's statement in his Epistle to the Romans:

> Sinners who do not have the law will perish without reference to it;
>
> …For it is not those who hear the law who are just in the sight of God; it is those who keep it who will be declared just.
>
> When Gentiles who do not have the law keep it as by instinct, these men although without the law serve as a law for themselves.
>
> They show that the demands of the law are written in their hearts.

Their conscience bears witness together with that law, and their thoughts will accuse or defend them on the day when, in accordance with the gospel I preach, God will pass judgment on the secrets of men through Christ Jesus. [2:12-16]

In the First Epistle to Timothy 4:10, its author, speaking for Paul, writes about "why we work and struggle as we do; our hopes are fixed on the living God who is the savior of all men, but especially of those who believe." In the same vein, Peter says in Acts 10:34-35: "I begin to see how true it is that God shows no partiality. Rather, the man of any nation who fears God and acts uprightly is acceptable to him." That was said in the context of gentile and Jew, but why wouldn't it apply to all different groups?

I think these passages are messages to us that God will judge all humankind in a fair and loving way. To my way of thinking, God is so loving that His mercy would not be limited to just those who have accepted Jesus Christ. What about those who never had an opportunity to know him? I believe God's judgment will be based on each individual's conduct, whether or not he or she was a Christian. I am confident his or her reward, salvation, or damnation, will be equitable without respect to religious beliefs or rites.

God will judge all in a fair and loving way.

Having said this, I am not proposing that we who are Christians should forget or forego our Christianity. What I'm saying is that we should not be smug about a supposed favored status and that we cannot earn our salvation by adherence to rigid codes of conduct. All of us are humans who are at some level flawed, imperfect, and unknowing. I believe God's judgment will be based on how well we have used the gifts He has given us in fulfilling His command to love our neighbors as ourselves—no matter who they are, what they believe, or how they worship Him. We should not despise those who are righteous just because they have customs and beliefs that differ from our own. We should support anyone who embodies God's message of loving unity because I believe God's judgment of each of us will include how much was done to both practice and spread that message.

Judgment Day

Christians have been waiting two thousand years for the Second Coming of Christ with its accompanying final judgment, and it's been reported that forty percent or so of American Christians think the final judgment day is not far off. In this belief, they are one with Peter, Paul, the other Apostles, and the early Christians. The first few generations of Christ's followers were absolutely certain that they had been promised this Second Coming in their lifetimes. It was to be in their near future and it would precede the fiery destruction of a flawed and pagan world with all of its inequities and iniquities. That belief gave them the strength to endure deprivation, persecution, and martyrdom.

Now we know that they were wrong. Our flawed world has struggled forward for two millennia with many Christians hoping year after year for the Second Coming in the manner they thought the Bible promised. Even though that en masse Judgment Day hasn't occurred, I'd suggest that Paul, the Apostles, and the evangelists were only partially incorrect in their transmission of God's message. They heard, as we hear, God through the filters of human needs, wants, and understanding. I am convinced that they were substantially right, but that their and others' interpretations through the ages as to when this event is to occur is where the boat was missed.

I am confident God will judge every human one at a time. But that takes place, perhaps, in a manner contrary to what we have been led over time to believe. In Luke 17:22-24, Jesus says,

> A time will come when you will long to see one
> day of the Son of Man but will not see it. They will tell

you he is to be found in this place or that. Do not go
running about excitedly.

The Son of Man in his day will be like the lightning
that flashes from one end of the sky to the other.

I think Jesus meant that judgment day will come to each of us
in an eye-blink instant and it will be all-consuming. And, as we read
in Mathew 24:44, "The Son of Man will come at the time you least
expect."

The Apostles believed Christ's promise that they would experience
his Second Coming in their lifetimes. And I think they did; it just
wasn't accompanied by the fiery termination of the whole world that
they had been expecting. They simply misunderstood how it would
occur; it was, instead, the visitation from God that takes place at the
end of everyone's corporal existence when personal judgment about the
way life was lived is rendered.

I'd ask you to consider whether or not there isn't more than
one lesson for us in this. As those closest to Christ both during and
immediately after his time here on Earth misinterpreted parts of his
teachings to them, we misunderstand his commands and message at
times to this very day.

The fact that God has not yet ended humanity's existence implies
that He has a good reason for allowing us to live. The challenge for each
of us is not one of predicting when Armageddon will come or in what
form God will appear. Rather, it is to prepare ourselves for whenever
the moment is that we are summoned for judgment. No matter what
one chooses to believe, one resurrection or many reincarnations, the
challenge is to discern the meaning and purpose of death. I believe
it defines life here on Earth, as God intends us to live it—bettering
ourselves until we're free from sin. We can live for the short time we are
here on Earth, or realize the hope of life after death. The challenge is
to triumph over sin. When it no longer exists, when it dies within our
souls, life will, indeed, be eternal.

NINE

Stagnate, or Evolve—
Expanding the Body of God

Paul teaches us that the advent of Christ and the Apostles' ministry to the gentiles was part of a larger plan that had been set in place by God. I have no reason to believe that His plan is now complete or is about to end. The ongoing revelations of that plan continue in our time and I'd contend that we are not close to its culmination. I am confident that, like those who came before us, our lives are intended to advance God's design and we're supposed to pass its glorious promise on to future generations.

History tells us that our development has been steady but that it's been slow, too. There are far more believers now than ever before, but there are still more who haven't come to God in any form. While the two millennia that have gone by since Christ lived may seem endless to many of us, they are but a blip on the eternal continuum of time as God measures it. Given this history, it seems only logical that God will allow a lot more time for humanity to continue its growth and get things right. How much more? Well, let us look at the setting God has provided for growth to occur—the Universe we discussed earlier—that gives us a good idea of God's timeframe.

Physicists and astronomers have argued whether this Universe of ours, with its billions of galaxies, is open-ended or closed. Will it continue to expand outward from its Big Bang origins, or stop at some point and contract upon itself, causing total destruction in a reverse Big Bang that cosmologists dub the Big Crunch? This debate hasn't been resolved but based on current science, the expansionist camp seems to be winning.

The one certainty in either scenario is that in several-hundred-billion years or so, all life in the Universe is doomed to extinction when the countless suns in the billions and billions of galaxies burn out or the Universe crunches back together into one solid mass. In either case, if we focus just on our own solar system, our period for growth in the future can go on for at least another four-to-six billion years until our Sol consumes itself and Earth. If we don't destroy ourselves before then as a result of ecological, nuclear, or biological holocaust, that is an incredibly long way into the future. As God's work has been meticulous in bringing us this far, I believe He wants us to focus on a much longer view than what, for Him, is the short span between Christ's resurrection and today.

Focus on a much longer view.

God wants our souls to evolve to a level that can survive for eternity and He will give us abundant opportunity to do so. If we take that long view, we won't break under the weight of our flaws and shortcomings. We can contribute to that distant future one day, and one soul, at a time.

I've observed that many of those who believe in God think of Him as a historic figure whose work was finished during Biblical times. He spoke then, and now it's just a matter of trying to live up to the words that were set in stone back then. Others limit His role in their lives by seeing Him as a God of the dead, not the living, and turn to Him when a loved one dies. Confronted with death, they pray to God and ask Him to take care of the deceased in the hereafter. He will, of course, do that. But we need to understand in our minds and in our hearts that He is equally concerned with those of us still here on Earth and all the future generations that will follow us. He is the God of the living, too, and I believe His greatest work is yet to be done.

Mankind has indeed been plodding along into its future, whether that began a million years ago or just yesterday. We may have advanced slowly in terms of social discourse, but advance we did—in action and in the words used for the codes that steer humanity's progress. God has guided us along the way, fitting His directions to each generation's needs and abilities.

God's greatest work is yet to be done.

I'd ask you to consider the striking contrasts between God's commands found in the Old Testament and the New. In many respects, they are so markedly different that atheists use them as proofs that God does not exist, and many theologians refer to an Old Testament God and a New Testament God as if He were two different entities. But He is not. He just uses the raw material—believers and non-believers alike—He has at a given time to advance His cause. God's commands to King Saul, as related in I Samuel 15, are instructive here. God ordered Saul to annihilate the city of Amalek; he was to kill all its people, livestock, and King Agag. Everyone and everything was doomed. Saul and his army attacked and destroyed that city and executed thousands of men, women, and children. But, skirting Divine commands, they saved the best of the cattle and sheep for later sacrifice and showed mercy to King Agag, sparing his life. We are told that God was furious with Saul for not carrying out His edicts to the letter and, in His wrath, withdrew support of Saul as king. He decreed that Saul and his lineage should be exterminated and replaced by David who would follow Divine instructions.

God changes His commands as conditions change.

Incredibly harsh treatment, I agree. But I believe God had a purpose during the time of Saul and David that required such ruthlessness. He wanted to ensure the uncontaminated survival of the Israelites and their unique concept of one righteous God to the exclusion of all others. The Israelites were a minuscule nation with a tenuous hold on this religious precept. They were in constant danger of being overwhelmed and then absorbed by the more numerous and more powerful peoples who surrounded them. The Israelites' one true God was under continuous threat of fading from human minds and hearts via assimilation into the pantheon of other gods worshiped by those neighbors. God couldn't let that happen; He wanted the Israelites' system of values and religious thought to survive for the generations that would follow, so He had to utilize harsh methods.

Does this mean that God wished mankind's later generations to act in similarly ruthless and brutal ways? I think not. Instead, when the time was right and such ruthlessness was no longer needed for God's purposes, He gave us Christ to teach us to love our neighbors, not massacre them.

Thus, it appears to me that God changes His teachings and commands to us as our conditions change in each subsequent future. These new prescriptions are always meant to advance His ultimate purpose—a mankind unified in greater perfection under Him.

But rather than sharing God's focus on what could be, many of us cup our hands to our ears in an attempt to catch the echoes of what God has said to humanity in ages gone by. We try to live up to a past ideal of purity. However, just as peoples, institutions, and laws evolve, I believe that how we define purity changes over time as well. And the words we now use will be as imperfect and as subject to improvement as the ones long ago proved to be. By looking back to what was an imperfect past, we fail to hear or heed what God is saying in the here and now about how we're supposed to help change the future He gives us.

We can mold the future we hope for.

That is not to say our past is to be ignored. Rather, it should be used to correct prior errors and thereby guide us toward the ideal of unity. But it serves no purpose to dwell on the past, long for it, or get angry about it, no matter how "pure" or unjust we've deemed it to be. The past cannot be changed; it is the future we can mold into the better whole we hope for.

I am convinced we have to set aside much of the past and come to grips with modern realities. Today, the effects of our errors can be so devastating in such short periods of time that we must use our collective knowledge to avoid them. We must heed the current messages God sends to us in the devastations that proliferate around the world, devastations that result from selfish pursuits. If that requires modification of well-intentioned but outmoded commands of former religious leaders, so be it. God will let us know if we take a wrong turn.

I'm also convinced that we do not exist merely to experience the here and now like the rest of the species who occupy the planet with us do. God has given us the intelligence to learn that the present is not what matters most. I would argue that the most important aspect of mankind's existence is a collective future. And if what is to come is the focus, then we are responsible for humanity's tomorrow and all the days that follow. If we recognize that what we do today has far-reaching impact, we'll make better choices in everything we do.

What we do today has far-reaching impact.

Had the Christians of two thousand years ago succumbed to their hardships and persecution by giving up their faith, we would not have had a great religion that has done, and continues to do, an awful lot of good. The same could be said for early Buddhists and followers of

Islam. Just as the gift of belief was protected and passed on to us, our challenge is to preserve the essence of what God stands for and pass it on to as many current and future people as is possible.

The Hope of a Long-Range View

Obviously, we cannot be certain how God views time or its passage, but we have some hints. The overwhelming evidence and scientific facts demonstrate that the Universe we know was created some 13.7 billion years ago in that cataclysmic instant referred to as the Big Bang. After that initial explosion, matter coalesced and was thrust outward into the vast expanse of space to form and reform into a hundred-plus billion galaxies with their vast number of stars and planetary bodies that astronomers and cosmologists study.

In the course of these celestial comings and goings 4.5 billion years ago, matter combined to produce our solar system and the planet we call Earth on which the first life forms appeared about two billion years later. Homo-sapiens—humans—didn't show up until another two billion years had gone by, about 350,000 years ago. Such timeframes are all but unfathomable to us; it's a struggle just to think in terms of recorded human history that spans less than ten-thousand years. As a result, when we consider God, we tend to cram Him and all of His works into that limited human timeframe. We try to fit God to what we know.

By His eternal timeframe, though, we can assume that when this Universe—the physical plant supporting all the life He created and what we call the cosmos—is finally played out, there will still be an endless amount of time to occupy Him. The almost incomprehensible lifetime of our Universe will have been just another dot on that timeline. What will He do then? God could start over again, I suppose. But despite our speculations, we don't know what He will do just as we do not know what He did before that Big Bang.

The point is that God has no reason to rush or to conform to human notions of when things should be done just because we are in a relative hurry. As hard as it is for those of us living today to comprehend this

God-ordained scale of time, despite all the scientific knowledge available to us, it must have been much harder for the author or authors of the Book of Genesis to do so. It describes Creation taking place over seven days. Those, however, could well have been God's version of "days" that were set against His eternal timeline. Only He knows how long they were. The concept of a day being equivalent to, say, a billion Earth years would have been all but unfathomable to whoever wrote Genesis, no matter how inspired they were by God Himself. Their sole point of reference was Earth days and that is the time description they recorded. They had no other alternative.

We try to fit God to what we know.

With the knowledge we have today, we are not as limited as our forefathers were. With full acknowledgment that our body of knowledge will be outdated some day, we should use it to connect the realities of the Universe around us to our march into the future toward God. When we contemplate the facts about time and space that are at our disposal, the conclusions we reach can expand our understanding of Him. For example, consider the ongoing battle between the proponents of Evolution and those who espouse the theory of Intelligent Design. What both sides to this debate refuse to recognize is that the two positions are not as mutually exclusive as they are wont to demand. The origin of life is not an either-or proposition. To get where we are today, God worked on a timescale of billions of years and used the laws of physics and quantum mechanics to build a Universe that can and does support life. In light of the proven age of the Universe and the vast billions of light-years it encompasses in space, there is absolutely no logical reason why we should believe that God was not prepared to use billions of years in evolutionary processes to grow life forms into what He wants them to be. If that process takes longer than the Bible suggests, so be it. God has eternity to work with, so why should He be in a rush?

The origin of life is not an either-or proposition.

But suggesting that God was willing to let evolution work is not the same as saying He did not and does not influence and guide that evolution. We now know that so many factors had to combine just so, one on top of another, for our Universe and life on Earth to evolve that the odds of all of them happening in just the right sequence and just the right way without intelligent design are miniscule.

To outline just a few of these factors, starting with the Big Bang, we can't ignore the fact that its explosion had to be exactly right in terms of the energy involved, the temperatures achieved and the gravitational forces produced. A little too much or too little of any of them, instead of a universe of expanding matter in the form of coalesced galaxies, there would be only a soup of atomic particles or wisps of nothingness. As Bill Bryson points out in *A Brief History of Nearly Everything*:

> [I]f the universe had formed just a tiny bit differently – if gravity were fractionally stronger or weaker, if the expansion had proceeded just a little more slowly or swiftly—then there might never had been stable elements to make you and me and the ground we stand on. Had gravity been a trifle stronger, the universe itself might have collapsed like a badly erected tent, without precisely the right values to give it the right dimensions and density and component parts. Had it been weaker, however, nothing would have coalesced. The universe would have remained forever a dull, scattered void.

Most scientists, including Richard Dawkins, author of *The God Delusion*, concede that as our Universe came into existence its controlling laws of physics and chemistry had to be, in Dawkins' words, "just right for yielding the richness of elements that we need for an interesting and life-supporting chemistry." And they were. Otherwise, we wouldn't be here. Had the Universe's component equations, forces, temperatures, and chemistry been just slightly different as they clearly could have been, life as we know it could not have formed or evolved. Again, there would have been no us.

Coming down to our local level, so to speak, if we consider just the circumstances of the planet we happen to inhabit, the Earth, we come face to face with other equally compelling facts. First, of course, is that there just happened to be an Earth-sized planet of just the right density and mass at just the right distance from the Sun for the formation of liquid water and then an oxygen-based atmosphere. And, this planet just happened to have a gravitational field with sufficient strength to retain that atmosphere once it was created. If our planet had settled, say, five percent nearer the Sun or fifteen percent farther away, it would not have been inhabitable; it would not support life. If the Earth had the mass of Mars, which is half the size of Earth but has only one-tenth of its mass, our home planet would have been unable to hold that atmosphere in place. On top of these developments, it just so happened that our world was blessed with a molten iron core at its center. In combination with the Earth's rotation, this core produces an immense magnetic field—a magnetosphere—that enshrouds the Earth, though it can't be seen with the naked eye. The magnetosphere's lines of force act as a *Star Wars*-like shield, protecting all life from the Sun's violent solar winds that would otherwise blast across us and sterilize everything.

The list of improbabilities that produced the Earth and its inhabitants more than hints at Intelligent Design.

Then there's the fact that our planet is also guarded by the gas giants—Jupiter, Saturn, Uranus and Neptune—that revolve in orbits more distant from the Sun than our own. These gigantic planets absorb or deflect, via their gravitational "slingshots," much of the punishing rain of asteroids and comets that might otherwise devastate our frail little Earth. Despite these guardians, at just the right moment in time asteroids did get through and smashed into our planet with an impact of such cataclysmic magnitude that extinction events occurred. World-shattering explosions wiped out the dinosaurs and that allowed the development and evolution of fragile mammals that wouldn't have otherwise survived and evolved. Thus, Man was able to arrive on the scene eons later.

The list of improbabilities that have produced the here and now is much more extensive than those I've covered here. In their totality, they lead me to the conclusion that there is more than ample suggestion of intelligence and control in the process that has produced the Universe, our planet, and us.

A rejection of Intelligent Design without an acknowledgment that this suggested intelligence just might exceed our ability to measure or detect it, raises the distinct question of a lack of intellectual honesty bordering on the doctrinaire. It reveals an artificial limitation of the mind that might be selective, too, in that such a mind often has no problem believing in other things that cannot be quantified but exist nonetheless, such as Adam Smith's "invisible hand," national pride, team spirit, and love.

We should not limit a limitless God.

Yet, atheists aver that if God cannot be understood, He cannot be. As I witnessed in more courtrooms than I care to count, it's impossible to prove a negative through affirmative evidence. The circumstantial evidence, however, as it relates to God is far more than what has been used to successfully make many other courtroom cases.

Once again, we should not try to limit a limitless God; what we should do is expand our horizons to take in God's frames of reference. Those include endless time, endless space, and, most important, endless love. As I've said, we insignificant humans can't be the center of the Universe or of God's focus. In the context of vast time and space, our physical bodies don't amount to all that much. How could they, in light of all the celestial matter and energy that dwarfs us? I suspect they don't count for much with God, either, especially in terms of shape, number of limbs, gender, skin color, and so many other things we think of as important. What does matter is the evolution of the attributes of spirit housed in those bodies, the spirit that mirrors Him.

What matters is the evolution of spirit.

I believe Darwinian evolution is a part of the way God works. For example, why should Neanderthals die out and Homo-sapiens survive and thrive? The great apes still live, so why not Neanderthals? To me, it confirms His Intelligent Design, not only of physical and cognitive traits, but of interpersonal traits that survive no matter what—love, honesty, caring, and commitment. I believe, too, that this evolutionary process of supposed random events is far from over and is one we can have an impact on. While there is much that is beyond our control, we should be wise about the events we select to influence and how we go about doing that. It behooves us to always keep in mind that the whole is greater than the sum of its parts. That's true about marriage and family, it's true about business organizations and church congregations, and it's also true about eternal time and life.

The challenge, again, is how we use the mere hours we have as opposed to the eternity God works with. Will we evolve by intelligently using the facts we know about the far-reaching Universe—and about the one within our grasp? What significance will our life have that lasts beyond the physical plane? What contribution will we make to the substance that attracts others to the ever-expanding body of God?

TEN

Lip Service, or Action—
Setting the Example

M odern astrophysicists and cosmologists have come to the startling conclusion that there are incredible but undetectable forces and gigantic amounts of unseen matter at play in our Universe that dominate its history, development, and future. These are referred to as "dark energy" and "dark matter." Modern science can only detect and measure them indirectly because of their aggregate effects; the celestial bodies we can see behave in a manner that could only be explained by the existence of these "dark" entities. We only know that they have to be there because our Universe would not function as it does otherwise. Whatever they are, Richard Panek, writing in the *New York Times Magazine*, suggests they are not "normal." According to him, to prove the existence of these dark entities, "the next round of evidence will have to be not only beyond anything we know but also beyond anything we know <u>how</u> to know."

When scientists were finally able to measure the speeds at which galaxies such as our own Milky Way rotated about their central axes, they came to the startling realization that every galaxy was revolving at such high rates, they ought to fragment and fly apart. There simply wasn't enough visible matter in the forms of suns, moons, planets, and stellar dust in those galaxies to generate sufficient gravitational forces to hold them together. The only possible answer to the puzzle was that each galaxy had to contain far more matter than we humans could see or detect with any of our measuring tools. It turned out that the stuff we can't detect is ninety-six percent of the total mass that's out there!

"Dark" stuff makes up ninety-six percent of the Universe.

Dr. Joel R. Primack and Nancy Ellen Abrams clarify these numbers even further. In their book, *The View From the Center of the Universe*, the authors explain that of the totality of the Universe's matter and energy, only 0.01% is made up of visible atoms, the solid stuff you and I know; 0.5% is made up of hydrogen and helium and 4% is "matter that is invisible in fact, but not in principal."; 25% of the total is cold, dark matter, and the balance of 70% is dark energy.

Mr. Panek explained why such an overwhelming amount of matter can't be detected or further qualified:

> To account for the dark-matter deficit, this material would have to be so massive and so numerous that we couldn't possibly miss it [if it were the normal stuff we are made of.]
>
> Which leaves <u>abnormal</u> matter, or what physicists call nonbaryonic matter, meaning that it doesn't consist of the protons and neutrons of "normal" matter. What's more (or perhaps more accurately, less), it doesn't interact at all with electricity or magnetism, which is why we wouldn't be able to see it, and it can only rarely interact even with protons and neutrons, which is why

trillions of these particles might be passing through you every second without you knowing it.

Modern particle physicists are expending vast sums of money and effort on sprawling particle accelerators—structures that wind over miles of terrain—in their efforts to detect and identify dark matter particles. So far, however, they haven't succeeded, even though they are sure the dark particles are there.

Similarly, dark energy first came to light when astronomers determined that the expansion of our universe was not, as they had expected, slowing down because of the gravitational pull of the vast mass of matter we've just discussed. It was, instead, accelerating. And if that wasn't puzzling enough, bodies at the far reaches of outer space were moving away from their Big Bang points of origin at an ever-increasing rate of speed. Something was stepping on the gas pedal, so to speak. We don't know what this force is or how it works, but we sure know that it is as real as wind in our face is.

Modern scientists are tearing their hair out trying to solve the mystery of what this dark stuff is that makes up the overriding bulk of the Universe. Some believe the answers to these puzzles are just around the corner. Others declare that it will take a new Einstein or Newton to ferret them out. In *The God Delusion*, Richard Dawkins suggests:

> It is an essential part of the scientific enterprise to admit ignorance, even to exalt in ignorance as a challenge to future conquests...Most scientists are bored by what they have already discovered. It is ignorance that drives them on.

So, in our ignorance we are trying to grapple with things that affect us even though they can't be seen, felt, or individually detected. I would suggest that the same thing can be said about God. We can't detect, define with certainty, or truly understand Him. But we can infer His existence from His impact on the separate lives of individuals and on humanity as a whole. Thus, like Dawkins' scientists, I think we should admit our ignorance and even exalt in it. It should be a challenge to drive us on to discover God and His purpose for us. The understanding of dark matter and dark energy may well turn out to be proverbial pieces of cake in comparison to an understanding of God, but that does not mean we should just stand pat and not reach for Him.

Exalt in recognized ignorance.

Dawkins prides himself on being a scientist and thinking like one. He derides theists who attribute anything that can't be explained to God. He takes the contrary position, declaring that because he cannot explain or solve the mystery of God, God can't exist. In doing so, he violates his own rule for what it means to be a scientist, which is to exalt in recognized ignorance and utilize it as a goad to consider the possible (if not probable), and keep looking.

Dawkins and I do see eye-to-eye on any number of proven facts and concepts. We both agree on the occurrence of the Big Bang and the Universe's thirteen-plus billion years of evolution since that seminal event. We agree that the Universe is governed by exquisitely-proportioned laws of physics and chemistry that had to be exactly right to produce us. We both embrace the Darwinian laws of evolution and natural selection that have led to the incredible diversity of interlocking life blanketing this planet of ours, which just happens to be positioned in exactly the right spot in our solar system to permit the development of that life. I would imagine that we would both acknowledge that there has to be both dark matter and dark energy dominating our Universe, even though modern science can't detect or understand their makeup. We just view these facts from different perspectives and draw different conclusions from them. In the end, it is the non-provable that separates us. Though he can't prove that God doesn't exist, it is Dawkins' profound faith that He does not. And though I can't scientifically prove He does exist, I am convinced He does.

Darkness and Light

Once again, rather than concentrate on differences, I prefer to build upon shared points of view. Dawkins and I agree on the inexorable progress of physical matter that resulted in the Earth and the Evolution of Species. I believe that God has used evolution as His tool in His ordering of the Universe. He has developed it over tens of billions of years, from matter and initial points of explosive energy to what surrounds us now. He shepherded life on Earth from a soup of single cells to the vast interlocking complex of life forms that now covers the face of our planet and permeates the depths of its oceans. As part of this, He shepherded us into existence. We, in turn, may not be able to control the mysterious aspects of natural selection, but we can control how we evolve as individuals. And that's what God had in mind when he first set the wheels of Creation in motion and kept them greased along the way.

On a human scale, God also shepherds the evolution of our knowledge, philosophy, social structures, and faiths. I've come to believe He wants all of these to be more flexible so they connect more and more people in loving, supportive ways. I would suspect that is especially true about faith. It's inconceivable that God would allow faith to inhibit or restrain spiritual evolution. Quite the contrary, it seems to me He intends faith to be an accelerant of spiritual growth just as dark energy accelerates the Universe's expansion. We can't explain faith, can't be certain how it works, but we detect it all around us in the purest souls who embody its essence. It's there, it's here, it's real. It exists. As does the God Who is behind everything.

We can control how we evolve as individuals.

As part of the evolutionary process, I believe that we are partners with God, engaged together in directing humanity's march to the future. Ours, I'm convinced, is an endeavor designed to produce the end result of an evolved humanity worthy of an eternal relationship with each other and with Him. The question then becomes, how do we do our part in steering toward that result? The answer I'd propose is that our job is to make the best possible choices we can in both our day to day and societal lives. We can opt to pay attention to the things that are right before our eyes, instead of putting blinders on, muddling through, and missing the abundant opportunities to effect positive change that are set before us.

I once read that a villain sees himself as the hero of his own tale. The conclusion I draw from that is we humans should constantly remind ourselves that it is very easy for us to ignore the facts and convince ourselves that, by God, we are in the right. We think we are the heroes of the tale and all those other folks are the villains. Of course, we are absolutely correct in our judgments at times. When the world is faced with a Hitler or apartheid, the assessment of right and wrong is obvious even if Hitler and the proponents of racial oppression see themselves as the heroes of their own stories. However, in the vast majority of cases, truth is far more nuanced and murky. It hides somewhere out there in the future we are groping towards in what I'm convinced isn't a straight line.

We are partners with God.

Allow me to offer the stark example of the defeat of Hitler and Nazi Germany. Many Americans have the idea that our country won World War II with only a little help from the British and other Europeans who, after letting Hitler spring up in the first place, held the fort until we could get there and straighten things out. Many do acknowledge that the Russians also fought the Germans, but as they were part of another evil empire under Stalin, those who want to ignore the war's eastern front dismiss these contributions to the victorious outcome; the U.S. just ended up saving them, too.

The truth is that the Russians, Ukrainians, and all the other peoples of the Soviet Union did more than we did to defeat Hitler. And they paid a far bloodier price than we in the West did, with losses of over twenty million lives, including more than seven million military dead. What these peoples did and the sacrifices they made in lives and resources could only have occurred under a brutal dictatorship like the one crafted by Joseph Stalin and his henchmen. Without it, they probably would have folded in the same way a number of the West's democracies had. Instead, they stayed together under extreme duress—just like the Israelites had—to defeat a formidable adversary. I wonder if we in America could have withstood the privation, mutilation, death, and material destruction the Soviets suffered. If nearly twenty percent of our population were killed and another thirty percent were injured or starving, would we have stayed in the fight? In such circumstances, what would the pressures to surrender have been like? As free-voting citizens, what would we have chosen to do then?

God utilized what He had at hand including the Soviet Union.

Only in a brutal society like the Soviet dictatorship where there was no choice other than being shot by your own side if you faltered could such sacrifices have been sustained. On the war's eastern front, the Soviets engaged in bitter, brutal fighting against well over one-hundred-eighty of Nazi Germany's best divisions that had more than two million German soldiers. Combined, the two sides lost more than one million men in the battle for Stalingrad alone.

Had Soviet Russia fallen and had those one-hundred-eighty Nazi divisions been available to defend the European coastline, it's probable that there would have been no Normandy invasion. The best we could have hoped for was a stalemate in Europe and victory in the Pacific over Japan. The Nazis would have finished the development of an atomic bomb they were working on; the result would have been a nuclear Armageddon far, far more devastating than the destruction wrought by the conventional weapons of World War II. Extermination of the entire Jewish population in Europe would have been a foregone conclusion.

God used countervailing forces to preserve humanity.

This discussion is in no way intended to ignore or diminish the heroic efforts of the U.S. and its western allies. Just as German divisions were tied up on the eastern front, a sizable mass of Nazi troops and materiel was occupied in Western Europe and unable to be thrown at Stalin and the Soviets to overwhelm them. Nonetheless, on balance, the hideous price the then-Soviet Union paid to defeat Hitler was the critical weight thrown onto the scale of victory. It tipped the outcome in our favor.

In the face of the destructive decisions made by evil madmen like Hitler and the German people under his sway, God took advantage of the countervailing choices of another psychotic individual, Joseph Stalin, and the populaces he commanded with an iron fist that surpassed that of the Nazis' to, in the end, protect His advance of humanity.

Let's be clear—I'm no advocate for or admirer of Communism, the Soviet Union, or dictators like Joseph Stalin. Instead, I am only acknowledging the hard cold facts of the sacrifices that were forced upon the people under that dictatorship to the benefit of the rest of the world. And I see God's hand in those events. I think He allowed ruthless Communism to triumph over a moribund Czarist Russia because that was the way to defeat a greater evil He foresaw arising thereafter. God then maneuvered Stalin's system into a fifty-year decline that led to the collapse of Soviet Communism. Progress, albeit slow, incredibly painful, and far from a straight line.

God Is As He Was

I suggest that World War II, the downfall of Nazi Germany, the subsequent demise of the Soviet Union, and the victories we've achieved over fanaticism are examples of the Old Testament version of God. Despite what we might like to think, that aspect of our Deity has never gone away. If we present Him with enough bad choices, I am convinced He is quite capable of dooming entire peoples to overcome them. He does so not because He wants to or enjoys it, but because we have left Him with no other alternative if He is to continue pushing and pulling us onward towards His goal of a unified humanity.

Many people may shake their heads and say God just doesn't act that way. They can't bring themselves to believe their God could have chosen the brutality of Communism and the Soviet Union to work His will. But the Bible wasn't written just to teach the people of long ago; it was written for yesterday, today, and tomorrow. Its lessons of the first destruction of Jerusalem's Temple and of the Israelites' Babylonian exile sure sound like the lessons of WWII. Long ago, God used two absolutely brutal nations, Assyria and Babylonia, to work His will on the Israelites when they chose to backslide from His teachings. Jews of that period believed that such draconian methods were chosen intentionally by God, as can be seen in Isaiah 13:4-5, 9, and 47:5-6:

> I have commanded my dedicated soldiers, I have summoned my warriors, eager and bold to carry out my anger...
>
> Listen! The noise of kingdoms, nations assembled! The Lord of hosts is mustering an army for battle.
>
> They come from a far-off country and from the end of the heavens,
>
> The Lord and the instruments of his wrath to destroy all the land.
>
> Lo, the day of the Lord comes, cruel with wrath and burning anger;
>
> To lay waste the land and destroy the sinners within it!
>
> Go into darkness and sit in silence, O daughter of the Chaldeans,
>
> No longer shall you be called sovereign mistress of kingdoms.
>
> Angry at my people I profaned my inheritance,
>
> And I gave them into your hand; but you showed them no mercy.

We can look to God's use of the Romans as another example of how progress under God doesn't move in straight lines. Their pacification of the Mediterranean world—the *Pax Romana* that was ruthlessly imposed with such efficient brutality—coupled with another destruction of

Jerusalem and its Temple by the Roman Legions, resulted in the Jewish Diaspora that seeded Christianity in its wake. In doing so, Romans also legitimized the concept of one ruler, Caesar, dominating all nations, as opposed to each having its own independent king. That helped set the stage for the spread and acceptance of a belief in one God over all those same peoples, replacing their multiple gods.

There are better choices to be made in every era before its history is written.

I'm convinced God maneuvers events in a way that provides opportunities for us to make positive choices for both corporal and spiritual growth. When we don't do what our hearts tell us should be done, He has to utilize more drastic measures to achieve His ends, no matter the pain that causes us. If we choose to cure the pain that exists now, act in every way possible to alleviate the suffering and fulfill the needs of others, we can avoid much greater pain later on.

There are better choices to be made in every era before its history is written. But we've yet to overcome the tendency to forget history's lessons, even the ones that have been repeated time and time again. To paraphrase the words of Ursala K. LeGuin in her novel, *The Other Wind*, we spend our lives learning how to choose to do what we have no choice but to do.

The first enemy is oneself.

War and godlessness have different faces today, but in many respects we're as flawed as the ancient Israelites were. Just like them, if we don't give God positive alternatives, He will increase the strife we suffer now until many more of us make more spiritual choices more often to advance His purpose. Let us hope that in our sloth we don't have to experience a nuclear or environmental holocaust that would make all of mankind's sins and brutality to date look like a mere warm-up match. I'd suggest we heed God's command to love one another that's been repeated with eloquence many times over. History, whether written in the Bible or in textbooks, reminds us that there is no acceptable choice other than to try to do the right thing every time. In Micah 6:8, the prophet tells us: "You have been told O man, what is good and what the Lord requires of you: Only to do right and to love goodness, and to walk humbly with your God."

How We Serve God

The peoples of the twenty-first century are as disparate as the ones in Biblical times were, and the challenges we face now are as epic as any that came before. We are in a war to save the planet and the human race; it is a war in which there are no civilians, no neutrals, and no safe havens where one can sit it out. We are all on the front lines because the first enemy is oneself. Each of us has to win his or her battles against indifference, selfishness, fear, and hate, and become, as Jesus said, servants of one another. In Ephesians 5:21, Paul teaches us to "defer to one another out of reverence for Christ." We must all serve our common interests. Throughout his writings, Paul speaks of the obligation that masters and slaves, husbands and wives, and parents and children have to serve each other. He focuses on service; let us do the same.

However, let us understand that servant-hood is not blind obedience to the commands of another with a suspension of courage, reason, and judgment. Nor is it the fearful acquiescence to the physical, economic, or socio-political power of whatever conglomerates we belong to or are confronted by. Its true meaning is to be found in the Dalai Lama's description of the best relationship—one in which the love for another exceeds the need for another. Put another way, a relationship where we put the interests of others ahead of our own.

Servant-hood requires patience and listening. Those qualities lead to understanding of our place in the world, in the cosmos, and in God's plan. Sometimes, service to another is a simple matter of shutting up when the reflex to speak up presents itself. My wife, Pat, has spent the better part of twenty-seven years trying to teach me that. I can't count the number of times she has declared, "Would you *please* wait until I finish explaining before you start telling me how to fix the problem. All I really wanted to do was vent, anyway." It's a lesson I'm still learning.

We've yet to overcome the tendency to forget the lessons of history.

Toleration is a part of this patience as well, and it's a huge part of service to others. We are not supposed to serve only those we deem worthy of our service. I'm convinced the true measure of our worth is the way we interact with those whom God has placed in opposition to us. The challenge is to recognize the humanity we share with everyone.

Given the myriad beliefs, cultures, and peoples God has allowed to flourish, I think He is challenging us, as he has all who have come before, to get along and rise as a whole. History has proven that the alternative—individuals or cliques flailing away in selfish pursuits—has failed miserably. It's as useless as a struggle against quicksand and just as deadly. Our prime modern example is the world's environment. No one has the right to deliberately cause or prolong the suffering of others in search of profit, gambling humanity's future on the bet that global warming will not devastate the Earth in the next hundred years. We should not worship at the altar of material gain, or say we do not have to expend the money and resources to halt or reduce harmful climate effects as soon as possible because that would be too great a sacrifice. None of us has a right to such self-centered and ill-gotten gain. We mustn't place our desires for more profit, comfort, and pleasure right now over the greater need that others have to survive or over the future of humanity.

How we serve others defines our relationship with God.

God sent prophets to us so that He could speak to us and teach us in a form we could tolerate without being overwhelmed, but the trappings of religious belief aren't important. How we serve others defines our relationship with God. Jews, Christians, Muslims, Hindus, and a host of other groups developed religions or systems to acknowledge God by many names. Buddhists and other groups of believers use different means and concepts to refer to a Superior Entity. Contrary to a pop phrase of my youth, this is a case where the medium is *not* the message. The message is that we must take God and each other into our hearts.

In his Epistle to the Ephesians, Paul instructs, "Do not continue in ignorance, but try to discern the will of the Lord." [5:17] As another proof that lessons need to be taught over and over again if they are to be learned, a similar prescription was offered long before in the Old Testament Book of Hosea: "Let us know, let us strive to know the Lord...For it is love that I desire, and knowledge of God rather than holocausts." [6:3, 6] The need to learn this is as great today as it was thousands of years ago.

Act with purpose even on the smallest of scales.

A lifetime of inquiry has led me to conclude that belief in God and Christ, Mohammed, Buddha, or the Hindu Gods, and pious expressions—reading the Bible, Koran or other religious works, and regular attendance at religious services—aren't enough to spread peace and fulfillment in the world. Passive lip service will not advance God's plan for the ultimate unification of mankind. Debates over who or what speaks best for God are as useless as the proverbial one over how many angels can fit on the head of a pin is. A choice to passively acknowledge good isn't sufficient to gain salvation and eternal life. What is needed is the choice to act with purpose on the smallest scale so that the good we profess to care about sprouts more often and grows much wider into a societal whole. Ultimately, we must do it all together.

The challenge for all of us is to identify the apathy and evil within ourselves that isn't as obvious as that of Caesar, Hitler, Stalin, or Bin Laden. When the evil and apathy within is conquered and replaced with active love, there's hope that evil will cease to exist everywhere and love will be all that remains.

Let us begin!

If you would like to continue your exploration of

CHOICES
AND
Challenges

Please visit its website at: www.choicesandchallenges.net;

- Conversations with the author
- Share your thoughts on its themes
- Raise your own questions

AUTHOR BIOGRAPHY

Alan Greer, as a nationally recognized trial lawyer and political activist, has followed a lifelong quest to understand the human condition, our relationship to God and each other, as well as the meaning of our lives. Since graduating from Annapolis and serving in both submarines and a year in the Vietnam War, he has traveled the world, worked with the homeless, fought national political battles and been at the center of both the Watergate cases and the post 2000 Presidential election trials in Florida. All of this, in combination with his personal studies in science, religion and philosophy, has lead to the uniquely fascinating and provocative points of view presented in *Choices and Challenges*.

BUY A SHARE OF THE FUTURE IN YOUR COMMUNITY

These certificates make great holiday, graduation and birthday gifts that can be personalized with the recipient's name. The cost of one S.H.A.R.E. or one square foot is $54.17. The personalized certificate is suitable for framing and will state the number of shares purchased and the amount of each share, as well as the recipient's name. The home that you participate in "building" will last for many years and will continue to grow in value.

THIS CERTIFIES THAT

YOUR NAME HERE

HAS INVESTED IN A HOME FOR A DESERVING FAMILY

1985-2005

TWENTY YEARS OF BUILDING FUTURES IN OUR COMMUNITY ONE HOME AT A TIME

1200 SQUARE FOOT HOUSE @ $65,000 = $54.17 PER SQUARE FOOT
This certificate represents a tax deductible donation. It has no cash value.

Here is a sample SHARE certificate:

YES, I WOULD LIKE TO HELP!

I support the work that Habitat for Humanity does and I want to be part of the excitement! As a donor, I will receive periodic updates on your construction activities but, more importantly, I know my gift will help a family in our community realize the dream of homeownership. **I would like to SHARE in your efforts against substandard housing in my community!** *(Please print below)*

PLEASE SEND ME _____ SHARES at $54.17 EACH = $ $_____

In Honor Of: _____

Occasion: (Circle One)   HOLIDAY   BIRTHDAY   ANNIVERSARY

      OTHER: _____

Address of Recipient: _____

Gift From: _____   *Donor Address:* _____

Donor Email: _____

I AM ENCLOSING A CHECK FOR $ $_____ PAYABLE TO HABITAT FOR HUMANITY <u>OR</u> PLEASE CHARGE MY VISA OR MASTERCARD *(CIRCLE ONE)*

Card Number _____   Expiration Date: _____

Name as it appears on Credit Card _____   Charge Amount $ _____

Signature _____

Billing Address _____

Telephone # Day _____   Eve _____

PLEASE NOTE: Your contribution is tax-deductible to the fullest extent allowed by law.
Habitat for Humanity • P.O. Box 1443 • Newport News, VA 23601 • 757-596-5553
www.HelpHabitatforHumanity.org